SAGA

OF THE

SIOUX

SAGA
OF THE
SIOUX

An Adaptation from Dee Brown's

Bury My Heart at Wounded Knee

by Dwight Jon Zimmerman

SQUARE
FISH

HENRY HOLT AND COMPANY
NEW YORK

Adapting one of the benchmark histories of the American West for a younger audience was both a tremendous opportunity and a tremendous obligation. I am profoundly grateful for the help and support of a number of people. First and foremost among those is Linda Luise Brown, Dee Brown's daughter and head of his estate whose permission and encouragement made this edition possible. Sally Doherty and Rebecca Hahn provided invaluable guidance and suggestions in the many stages of the manuscript and image acquistion process. I must also thank Patrick Collins and Meredith Pratt for their enthusiasm and skill in turning the many raw elements into a polished book. I am grateful that my daughter, Léa Zimmerman, agreed to help her harried father and create the maps that are so essential in making clear the complex movements that occur during a battle. I am especially grateful to my agent, George Nicholson of Sterling Lord Literistic, whose support and dedication throughout this project never wavered. Finally, I must thank my wife, Joëlle, for her common sense and wisdom in yet another marathon effort of writing.

For a complete list of Dee Brown's original source material, see *Bury My Heart at Wounded Knee*, from which this book is derived. Sources for the Introduction and Epilogue include *Encyclopedia of the Great Plains*, David J. Wishart, editor (Lincoln: University of Nebraska Press, 2004); Republic of Lakotah website (www.republicoflakotah.com); *U.S. v. Dennis Banks*, 73-5034, 73-5062, 14, 15 (1974); *U.S. v. Russell Means*, 73-5035, 73-5063, 14, 15 (1974).

Image credits: pp. viii–ix, istockphoto 7667507 © Ken Canning; p. x, © Jim Cortez; p. 19, New Ulm map courtesy of the Library of Congress Geography and Map Division, Call # G4144.N4A3 1870 .R8 Rug 112; p. 75, Fort Philip Kearney map courtesy of Wikipedia; p. 142, postage stamp of Crazy Horse courtesy of the U.S. Postal Service. All other images courtesy of the Library of Congress Prints and Photographs Online Catalog; reproduction numbers are included with each caption.

Frontispiece: Prairie Chief, Edward S. Curtis, 1907

SQUARE
FISH

An Imprint of Macmillan
175 Fifth Avenue, New York, NY 10010
mackids.com

Library of Congress Cataloging-in-Publication Data
Brown, Dee Alexander.
Saga of the Sioux : an adaptation from Dee Brown's Bury My Heart at Wounded Knee /
[adapted by] Dwight Jon Zimmerman.
p. cm.
Includes bibliographical references.
ISBN 978-1-250-05067-0 (paperback) • 978-1-4668-8261-4 (e-book)
1. Indians of North America—Wars—West (U.S.) 2. Indians of North America—West (U.S.)
3. West (U.S.)—History. I. Zimmerman, Dwight Jon. II. Brown, Dee Alexander.
Bury my heart at Wounded Knee. III. Title.
E81.B754 2011 978—dc22 2011004792

Originally published in the United States by Henry Holt and Company
First Square Fish Edition: 2014
Book designed by Meredith Pratt
Square Fish logo designed by Filomena Tuosto

1 3 5 7 9 10 8 6 4 2

AR: 7.8 / LEXILE: 1140L

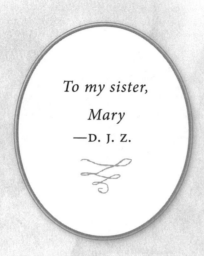

To my sister,

Mary

—D. J. Z.

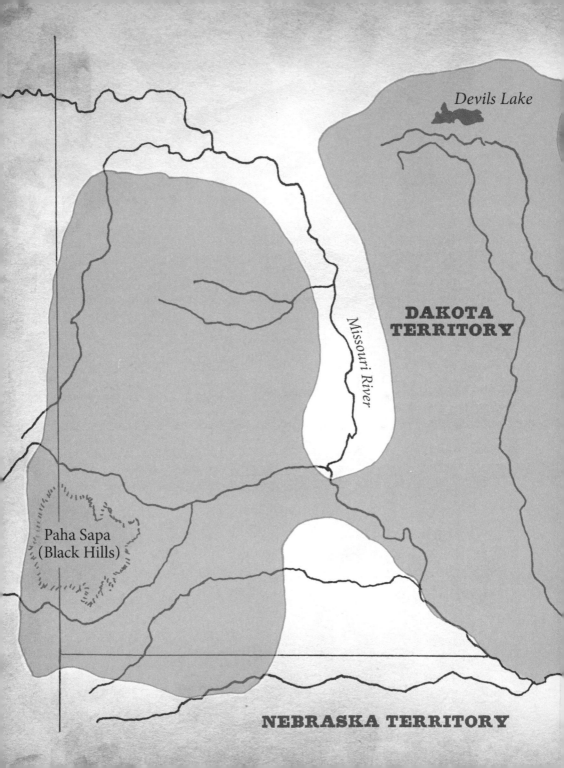

Devils Lake

DAKOTA
TERRITORY

Missouri River

Paha Sapa
(Black Hills)

NEBRASKA TERRITORY

Contents

Note to the Reader

WHEN EXPLORER CHRISTOPHER COLUMBUS landed on the Caribbean island of Hispaniola in 1492, he thought he had succeeded in reaching his goal of India. As a result, he called the natives he met "Indians." Even after he and other explorers discovered that they had actually found a new continent, the name stuck. In the late 20th century, the term Native Americans became a popular replacement in an effort to help correct this historical wrong. Today both names are used, a practice that is repeated here in *Saga of the Sioux*.

Misnaming errors also extended to the names of tribes and people. Two common reasons for this were the varied skills of the translators, and the prejudices of the people receiving the translation. For instance, *Sioux* is an English corruption of a French word based on a name used by the Sioux's old enemies the Ojibwa (you'll learn more about this on page 6). The most famous example of an individual being misnamed is the Sioux chief Man-Afraid-of-His-Horses. He was not afraid of his own horses. A more accurate translation would have been They-Fear-Even-His-Horses—meaning he was so dangerous in battle that just the sight of his horse inspired fear in his enemies. Perhaps if the original translator had recorded his name as

Men-Afraid-of-His-Horses, he would have avoided creating such a misimpression.

Spellings of Native American names may also differ among sources due to the challenge of documenting nonwritten languages.

Undoing the errors of centuries is beyond the power of this one book. For the sake of clarity and comprehension, the well-known names such as Man-Afraid-of-His-Horses and others are used in this text, and their spellings follow Dee Brown's original book.

A Ghost Dance ceremony.
[LOC, USZ62-3726]

Introduction

"HISTORY IS WRITTEN BY THE VICTORS," said British prime minister Winston Churchill. It's easy to understand why. The victors want to brag about their success. The surviving victims often don't want to talk about their defeat because the memory is too painful.

The history most people know about Indians is told from the point of view of the white people who conquered them. There's another reason for this. Almost all Native American tribes in North and South America did not have a written language. And human nature being what it is, the conquerors, from the Spanish conquistadors to the U.S. Cavalry, wrote about their heroic deeds and pretty much ignored the bad things that happened to the Indians.

That's why Dee Brown's book, *Bury My Heart at Wounded Knee: An Indian History of the American West*, is so important. When published in 1971, it was as if a thunderbolt had struck. It used as many primary sources as possible—interviews with Indian chiefs who fought the battles, government records, letters, diaries, articles, and other documents—to tell the Indians' side of the story from 1860 to 1890.

And what a sad story it is—a saga in which few white men are heroes. *Bury My Heart at Wounded Knee* revealed that an overwhelming number of white settlers, hunters, soldiers, and men of authority were arrogant, greedy, racist, murderous, and cruel beyond belief. To get Indian land, they lied, cheated, stole, and killed those Indians who crossed their paths, from warriors to innocent women, children, and the elderly. Today it is difficult, if not impossible, to understand how these people could have done what they did and feel no shame. But that's what happened—and not to just one tribe or nation. As *Bury My Heart at Wounded Knee* revealed, from sea to shining sea, it happened to them all.

Dee Brown's classic is a big and powerful work. Condensing the entire book into one volume for a younger audience ran the risk of distorting it through oversimplifying the facts and unfairly leaving out many important events. All tribes suffered similarly from United States government policies and its citizens. Though all were eventually defeated, one nation stood out as having fought the longest and most successfully.

That is why this adaptation focuses on one Indian nation from Dee Brown's book, the Sioux. As the largest and most powerful nation, the Sioux represent the story of the Native American experience in the American West. Their epic fight against the United States covered the entire three decades written about in *Bury My Heart at Wounded Knee*. Their leaders included some of the most famous warrior chiefs in Indian history: Red Cloud, the Sioux's greatest diplomat; Sitting Bull, the Sioux's greatest strategist; and Crazy Horse, the Sioux's greatest field general. The struggle to keep their land produced some of the most famous events in the Indian Wars: the Fetterman Massacre, the Battle of the Little Bighorn, the Ghost Dance, and finally, the Massacre at Wounded Knee.

In this retelling of the saga of the Sioux, details about events that don't directly deal with the Sioux story have been removed or condensed. Some extra information about people and locations mentioned in Dee Brown's original text has been added to help readers who may be unfamiliar with those individuals and the places where they lived, fought, and died. And some names, such as "Bozeman Trail" for "Bozeman Road," have been changed into a form more familiar to today's readers in order to reduce confusion. There are two new sections: the first chapter and the epilogue. The first chapter provides important background about the Sioux people. The epilogue summarizes what has happened to them since 1890. It contains some previously unpublished material from Dee Brown's files. It also briefly reveals the Sioux nation's ongoing epic struggle to keep its identity and tells how, eventually, they were able to achieve a measure of success against a federal government that had so often wronged them.

Because most people are more familiar with the English translation of Sioux names, those translations are used throughout to avoid confusion. But, in the case of important chiefs, their native-language names are also included.

In the 30th-anniversary edition of *Bury My Heart at Wounded Knee*, Dee Brown wrote, "We rarely know the full power of words, in print or spoken. It is my hope that time has not dulled the words herein and that they will continue through the coming generation to be as true and direct as I originally meant them to be."

In 2011, as *Bury My Heart at Wounded Knee* celebrates its 40th anniversary, it is my hope that *Saga of the Sioux* will inspire readers to want to know more about this tragic chapter in our history. And that they will continue this quest of discovery by reading *Bury My Heart at Wounded Knee*, as it remains a landmark history of the conquest of the West from the Native Americans' point of view.

—Dwight Jon Zimmerman

An undated Mathew Brady studio photograph (opposite) of a delegation of Sioux and Arapaho led by Chief Red Cloud in Washington, D.C. Indians in photo, from left to right: (seated) Red Cloud, Big Road, Yellow Bear, Young-Man-Afraid-of-His-Horses, and Iron Crow; (standing) Little Big Man, Little Wound, Three Bears, and He Dog. The white men are not identified. Note that Big Road, Young-Man-Afraid-of-His-Horses, and Iron Crow are wearing a large cross on their chests, indicating that they had converted to Christianity. Missionaries probably insisted they wear this large cross in order to publicize their success in converting important Sioux chiefs. [LOC, DIG-cwpbh -04474]

SAGA

OF THE

SIOUX

*An 1890 photograph by John C. H. Grabill of a group of Minneconjou Sioux from Big
Foot's village. The Sioux man in white man's clothing, standing fifth from the left and
wearing a badge on his chest, is a Sioux reservation police officer.* [LOC, DIG-ppmsc-02526]

Oceti Sakowin
("Seven Council Fires")
THE GREAT SIOUX NATION

When European settlers arrived in the New World of North and South America, they encountered a wide variety of Indian tribes that had made the land their home. Some Native American tribes were relatively small. Others had grown large enough to create a nation. Nations contained several tribes linked together through common languages, blood relations, and customs. Since Indians lived off the land, they usually separated into small bands, sub-bands, or subtribal units in order to make sure they could hunt and harvest enough food to eat. These subunits would regularly gather at sacred locations during the summer to perform religious ceremonies and discuss in council important matters affecting the nation.

These are the various groups that formed the Sioux Nation.

East
Santee *(Dakota speakers)*
Mdewakanton
Sisseton
Wahpekute
Wahpeton

Central
Wiciyelas *(Nakota speakers)*
Yankton
Yanktonais

West
Teton *(Lakota speakers)*
Blackfoot Sioux
Brulé
Hunkpapa
Minneconjou
Oglala
Sans Arcs
Two Kettles

ONE

Who Are the Sioux?

My friends, this country that you have come to buy is the best
country that we have . . . this country is mine, I was raised in it;
my forefathers lived and died in it; and I wish to remain in it.

—CROW FEATHER OF THE SANS ARCS SIOUX

PROBABLY THE MOST FAMOUS Native American people of North America, the Sioux gave to history one of the great images of the American West: a proud Plains warrior on horseback. But the Sioux are much more than just that image. The Great Sioux Nation, known as Oceti Sakowin, or "Seven Council Fires," is one of the largest tribal confederations in North America. In general, its people are identified by one of their three language dialects (Dakota, Nakota, Lakota), location (the eastern Santee, central or middle Wiciyelas, and western Teton), and more specifically by their individual band or sub-band (such as Yankton or Oglala). For instance, Chief Red Cloud could be identified any one of three ways: as a Teton because he lived in the westernmost part of Sioux land, as a

The Prairie Chief, *a photograph of a Sioux warrior on horseback taken by Edward S. Curtis around 1907. With the closing of the frontier in 1890, it was widely believed that Native Americans would soon be completely assimilated into white society and their traditional customs would vanish. This resulted in a movement, particularly in photographs, to record every aspect of Indian life before it was gone. Curtis was one of the great photographers of American Indians and of the American West. [LOC, USZ62-121906]*

Lakota because this was the dialect he spoke, or as an Oglala because he was a member of that sub-band. (See page 3.)

The name "Sioux" comes from what their enemies the Ojibwa called them: *Na dou esse*, which means "Snakelike Ones" or "Enemies." French traders, the first to encounter both nations, spelled the Ojibwa word *Nadousioux*. The English and American traders, who came later, shortened it to Sioux.

The Sioux originally lived along the southeast coast of North America—the Santee River in South Carolina got its name from the Santee Sioux. They were gradually pushed west by other tribes, like the Ojibwa, who were themselves pushed west by white settlers. By the 17th century, the Sioux had settled in the north-central section of the North American continent. Like many other Native American peoples, the Sioux were nomads.

The Indian of the Plains as He Was by Charles Marion Russell, one of the great contemporary artists and sculptors of the American West. Russell greatly admired the American Indians, and his illustrations of them are distinguished by their sensitive treatment. [LOC, USZ62-115207]

They were primarily hunters, though the eastern Santees also did some farming, with buffalo being their most important source of food.

Though the Sioux had chiefs who had individual leadership responsibilities (such as war chiefs), the important decisions that affected the tribe were always discussed in groups called councils. Councils included the chiefs, as well as medicine men and other respected members of the tribe. Council gatherings were always public affairs held in front of the rest of the tribe, and everyone had a right to speak.

An 1891 photograph by John C. H. Grabill of a young Oglala girl sitting in front of a tepee with her puppy. The smaller tepee on the left is probably a shelter for her dog. [LOC, USZ62-22970]

The most sacred land for the Sioux, particularly the Lakota, is Paha Sapa, the Black Hills of South Dakota. According to their tradition, it is there that Wakantanka, the Great Spirit, created them and gave them their sacred symbols and rites, including the Sun Dance.

At its height, the Great Sioux Nation stretched from Wisconsin and Minnesota to Montana and Wyoming, and from North

This 1907 Grabill photograph is titled War Preparation *and shows a reenactment demonstrating how Sioux warriors got ready before they rode off to fight. [LOC, USZ62-121907]*

Dakota to Iowa and Nebraska. They were proud, fierce, and feared warriors. It would take the United States government about 30 years to finally defeat them.

The opening battles of that campaign would begin in the eastern part of their territory, in the Santee land of Minnesota at the same time the United States was fighting the Confederacy in the American Civil War (1861–1865).

TWO

War Begins in Minnesota

*Yes; they fight among themselves, but if you strike at them they
will all turn on you and devour you and your women and little
children just as the locusts in their time fall on the trees and
devour all the leaves in one day.*
—LITTLE CROW OF THE SANTEE SIOUX

DURING THE 10 YEARS leading up to the Civil War, more
than 150,000 white settlers pushed into Santee country.
This was the result of two treaties signed in 1851: the Treaty
of Traverse des Sioux and the Treaty of Mendota. By agreeing
to the treaties, these woodland Sioux surrendered nine-tenths
of their land. They were crowded into two reservations, also
known as agencies: the Upper Sioux Agency near Granite Falls
and the Lower Sioux Agency near Redwood Falls. Both were on
the Minnesota River in southwest Minnesota. In return, the
Santee were guaranteed that this reservation land was theirs
forever, and they were supposed to receive cash and annual
payments called annuities totaling $2,806,000.

Because they had so little land left, the Santee were forced to
give up their traditional way of life and to learn how to farm
like the white man. This was something the government
wanted all along. Sixty-one-year-old Ta-oya-te-duta (Little Crow)
was one of the chiefs who signed the treaties. Little Crow was a
third-generation chief of the Mdewakanton. He had been to

Little Crow, a chief of the Santee Sioux and leader of the war against the white men in Minnesota in 1862. [LOC, USZ61-83]

Washington to see the Great Father, President James Buchanan, and had agreed to learn how to dress and live like a white man. He had joined their Episcopalian religion and started a farm. He had hoped that the Santee and the white men would be able to live together peacefully. But those hopes had been dashed.

Over the years, promised annuities did not always arrive on time. This forced the Santee to buy their food, clothing, and other goods on credit from traders authorized by the government to sell to the Indians. The Santee learned to hate the credit system because they had no control over the accounts. Traders would charge high prices. Sometimes they would cheat by saying they had sold the Santee supplies when they hadn't. When the Santee protested to the agents from the Office of Indian Affairs, the government agency responsible for Indian welfare, the agents sided with the traders.

In the summer of 1862, relations reached the breaking point. Drought had struck in 1861 and returned in 1862. With the Indians' crop yields so poor, many Santees had to buy food on credit. Earlier that summer the Lower Agency Mdewakantons took their growing resentment out on Little Crow, accusing him of betraying them when he signed away their lands by treaties. They elected Traveling Hail to be their speaker in place of Little Crow. Though Little Crow was still a chief, few of his own people now listened to him.

At the end of the month known to the Sioux as the Moon of the Red Blooming Lilies (July), several thousand Santees assembled in front of the warehouse and fort compound in the

Upper Sioux Agency to collect their annuities so that they might buy food. The money did not arrive. They heard rumors that the Great Council in Washington (Congress) had spent all their money fighting the Civil War and could not send anything to the Indians. Little Crow and some of the other chiefs went to their agent, Thomas Galbraith. They asked him to issue food from the agency warehouse, which was filled with provisions.

Galbraith replied that he could not do this until the money arrived. He posted 100 soldiers from the nearby fort to guard the warehouse. It was in the Moon When the Geese Shed Their Feathers (August) that the Santee decided they had waited long enough. On August 4, some 500 armed Santee warriors surrounded the soldiers. Other warriors broke into the warehouse and began carrying out food. The white soldier chief, Timothy Sheehan, sympathized with the Santees. Instead of shooting them, he persuaded Galbraith to issue food to the Indians and await payment from the government. After Galbraith did this, the Santees left peacefully. Little Crow did not leave for his home until the agent promised to issue similar amounts of food to the Santees at the Lower Agency.

Early on August 15, Little Crow and several hundred hungry Mdewakanton assembled at the Lower Agency. It soon became obvious that Galbraith and the four traders had no intention of issuing food before the arrival of the annuity funds.

An angry Little Crow arose, faced Galbraith, and spoke. "We have waited a long time. The money is ours, but we cannot get it. We have no food, but here are these stores, filled with food.

We ask that you, the agent, make some arrangement by which we can get food from the stores, or else we may take our own way to keep ourselves from starving."

Galbraith turned to the traders and asked them what they would do. Trader Andrew Myrick declared, "So far as I am concerned, if they are hungry let them eat grass or their own dung."

Myrick's words angered all the Santees, but to Little Crow they were like hot blasts upon his already seared emotions. For years he had tried to keep the treaties, to follow the advice of the white men, and to help his people learn how to live like white men. Little Crow knew that Myrick's words would destroy what little respect Little Crow still had among the Santee.

In the old days he could have regained leadership by going to war, but the treaties pledged him not to engage in hostilities with either the white men or other tribes. Why was it, he wondered, that the Americans talked so much of peace between themselves and the Indians, and between Indians and Indians, and yet they themselves waged such a savage war with the Graycoats (Confederates) that they had no money left to pay their small debts to the Santees? He knew that some of the young men in his band were talking of war against the white men to drive them out of the Minnesota Valley. It was a good time to fight the whites, they said, because so many Bluecoat soldiers were away fighting the Graycoats. Little Crow considered such talk foolish. He had been to the East and seen the power of the Americans.

On Sunday, August 17, Little Crow attended the Episcopal

Church at the Lower Agency and listened to a sermon delivered by the Reverend Samuel D. Hinman. Reverend Hinman had established his church at the agency in 1860 and had learned the Sioux language. His mission in life was to convert all the Sioux to Christianity and make them live like white men. At the conclusion of services, Little Crow shook hands with the other worshippers and returned to his house. It was the last time he attended Reverend Hinman's church.

Late that night Little Crow was awakened by the sound of many voices and the noisy entry of several Santee. Chiefs Shakopee, Mankato, Medicine Bottle, and Big Eagle came in, along with four frightened young warriors. The group said they had also summoned Chief Wabasha because they needed to hold an emergency council. As soon as Wabasha arrived, the group began to speak.

Earlier in the afternoon, four hungry young men from Shakopee's band had crossed the river that was the border of the reservation to hunt in the Big Woods near Acton Township, which now belonged to white men. Something very bad then happened. Big Eagle explained,

> They came to a settler's fence, and here they found a hen's nest with some eggs in it. One of them took the eggs, when another said, "Don't take them, for they belong to a white man and we may get into trouble." The other was angry, for he was very hungry and wanted to eat the eggs, and he dashed them to the ground and replied, "You are a coward.

You are afraid of the white man. You are afraid to take even an egg from him, though you are half-starved. Yes, you are a coward, and I will tell everybody so." The other replied, "I am not a coward. I am not afraid of the white man, and to show you that I am not, I will go to the house and shoot him. Are you brave enough to go with me?" The one who had called him coward said, "Yes, I will go with you, and we will see who is the braver of us two." Their two companions then said, "We will go with you, and we will be brave, too." They all went to the house of the white man, but he got alarmed and went to another house where there were some other white men and women. The four Indians followed them and killed three men and two women. Then they hitched up a team belonging to another settler and drove to Shakopee's camp . . . and told what they had done.

On hearing of the murders of the white people, Little Crow scolded the four young men. Then he asked Shakopee and the others why they had come to him for advice when they had chosen Traveling Hail to be their spokesman. The leaders assured Little Crow that he was still their war chief. No Santee's life would be safe now after these killings, they said. It was the white man's way to punish all Indians for the crimes of one or a few. The Santees might as well strike first instead of waiting for the soldiers to come and kill them. It would be better to fight the white men now while they were fighting among themselves far to the south.

Little Crow rejected their arguments. The white men were too powerful, he said. Yet he admitted the settlers would exact bitter vengeance because women had been killed.

Then one of the young braves cried out, "Ta-oya-te-duta is a coward!"

Little Crow replied, "Ta-oya-te-duta is not a coward, and he is not a fool. Braves, you are like little children; you know not what you are doing."

Little Crow added, "Kill one—two—ten, and ten times ten will come to kill you. Count your fingers all day long and white men with guns in their hands will come faster than you can count. . . . Yes; they fight among themselves, but if you strike at them they will all turn on you and devour you and your women and little children just as the locusts in their time fall on the trees and devour all the leaves in one day."

But because of the 10 years of broken treaties and broken promises, he understood why they wanted to fight. Though he knew it was a war the Santees could not win, Little Crow finally agreed they must fight. He then repeated, "Ta-oya-te-duta is not a coward; he will die with you." The Santee chiefs promised to gather their warriors for battle. Then they and the four young warriors left.

Little Crow sent messengers upstream to summon the Wahpetons and Sissetons to join in the war. The women were awakened and began to make bullets while the warriors cleaned their muskets. The war that would be called Little Crow's War was about to begin.

One of the chiefs who participated in the war was Big Eagle.

Years later, he recalled that Little Crow gave orders to attack the Lower Agency trading post early the next morning and "kill all the traders." When the force started to attack the agency's trading post, he said, "I went along. I did not lead my band, and I took no part in the killing. I went to save the lives of two particular friends if I could. I think others went for the same reason, for nearly every Indian had a friend he did not want killed; of

This map of the south half of Minnesota shows the important landmarks and battles in Little Crow's War.

course he did not care about anybody else's friend. The killing was nearly all done when I got there."

One of the dead was Andrew Myrick. Someone had stuffed his mouth with grass. Big Eagle recalled the warriors saying, "Myrick is eating grass himself."

The Santees killed 20 men, captured 10 women and children, emptied the warehouses of provisions, and set the other buildings afire. The remaining 47 inhabitants (some of whom were aided in their escapes by friendly Santees), including Reverend Hinman, fled across the river to Fort Ridgely, 13 miles downstream.

On the way to Fort Ridgely, the survivors met a company of 45 soldiers marching to the aid of the agency. Reverend Hinman warned the soldiers to turn back. The soldier chief, John Marsh, refused to heed the warning and marched into an ambush. Only 24 of his men escaped.

Encouraged by this success, Little Crow decided to attack Fort Ridgely. By this time, Wabasha and his band had arrived, Mankato's force had also been increased by more warriors, and fresh allies were reported to be on their way.

During the night, these chiefs and their several hundred warriors moved down the Minnesota Valley. Early on the morning of August 19, they began assembling on the prairie west of the fort.

When some of the young warriors who had never been in battle before saw the sturdy stone buildings of the fort and the armed Bluecoats waiting there, they had second thoughts. While traveling down from the Lower Agency, they had talked of how easy it would be to raid the nearby village of New Ulm. It was filled with stores to be looted, and no soldiers were there.

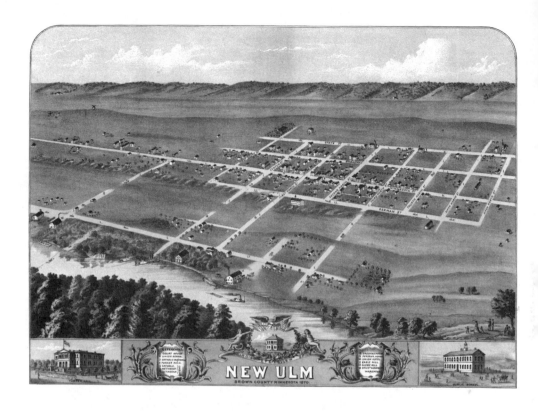

NEW ULM
BROWN COUNTY MINNESOTA 1870.

Why not fight at New Ulm? Little Crow told them the Santees were at war, and to be victorious they must defeat the Bluecoat soldiers. If they could drive the soldiers from the valley, then all the white settlers would go away. The Santees would gain nothing by killing a few white people in a village.

But the young men decided to attack New Ulm anyway. Once they had left, Little Crow's force was too weak to attack Fort Ridgely. He consulted with the other chiefs, and they decided to delay the assault until the next day.

That evening the young warriors returned from New Ulm. Their attack had failed. They had frightened the people

A map of New Ulm, Minnesota, looking southwest, published in 1870, eight years after the end of Little Crow's War. In the foreground is the Minnesota River.

19

there, they said, but the town was too strongly defended. Also a bad lightning storm struck in the afternoon. Everyone's attention was now on the attack of Fort Ridgely. About 400 warriors were assembled for the assault. Lightning Blanket, a participant, later said,

We started at sunrise and crossed the river at the agency on the ferry, following the road to the top of the hill below Faribault's Creek, where we stopped for a short rest. There the plans for attacking the fort were given out by Little Crow. . . .

After reaching the fort, the signal, three volleys, was to be given by Medicine Bottle's men to draw the attention and fire of the soldiers, so the men on the east [Big Eagle's] and those on the west and south [Little Crow's and Shakopee's] could rush in and take the fort.

We reached the Three Mile Creek before noon and cooked something to eat. After eating we separated, I going with the footmen to the north, and after leaving Little Crow we paid no attention to the chiefs; everyone did as he pleased. Both parties reached the fort about the same time, as we could see them passing to the west, Little Crow on a black pony. The signal, three shots, was given by our side, Medicine Bottle's men. After the signal the men on the east, south, and west were slow in coming up. While shooting we ran up to the building near the big stone one. As we were running in we saw the man with the big guns [cannons], whom we all knew, and as we were the only ones in sight he shot into us, as he had gotten ready after hearing the shooting in our direction. Had Little Crow's men fired after we fired the signal, the soldiers who shot at us would have been killed. Two of our men were killed and three hurt, two dying afterward. We ran back into the creek and did not know whether the other men would come up close or not, but they did and the big guns drove them back from that direction. If we had known that they would come up close, we could have shot at the same time and killed all, as the soldiers were out in the big opening between the buildings. We did not fight like white men with one officer; we all shot as we pleased. The plan of rushing into the buildings was given up, and we shot at the windows, mostly at the big stone building, as we thought many of the whites were in there.

We could not see them, so were not sure we were killing any. During the shooting we tried to set fire to the buildings with fire arrows, but the buildings would not burn, so we had to get more powder and bullets. The sun was about two hours high when we went around to the west of the fort, and decided to go back to Little Crow's village and come and keep up the fighting next day.

That evening in the village, both Little Crow and Big Eagle were in low spirits because they had not been able to take the fort. Big Eagle was against making another attack. The Santees did not have enough warriors, and they would lose too many men if they tried it. Little Crow said he would decide later what to do. Meanwhile everyone should go to work preparing for battle just in case.

Later in the evening, 400 Wahpeton and Sisseton warriors arrived from the Upper Agency. Little Crow was elated. The united Santee Sioux, 800 strong, were surely enough warriors to take Fort Ridgely. He called a war council and issued orders for the next day's fighting.

This time, instead of approaching the fort boldly, the Santee warriors fastened prairie grass and flowers to their headbands as a means of concealment. They then crept up the gullies and crawled through the brush until they were close enough to fire upon the defenders. A shower of blazing arrows set roofs afire; then the Santees rushed the stables. For a few minutes there was hand-to-hand fighting around the stables, but again the Santees had to give way before fierce blasts of the soldiers' artillery.

Little Crow was wounded—not seriously, but the loss of blood weakened him. When Little Crow withdrew from the field to regain his strength, Mankato led another assault. But heavy cannon fire cut down the rushing warriors, and the attack failed.

Late in the afternoon the Santee leaders called off the attack. Lightning Blanket said later, "Some wanted to renew the attack on the fort the next morning and then go to New Ulm; others wanted to attack New Ulm early the next morning and then come back and take the fort. We were afraid the soldiers would get to New Ulm first."

The soldiers that Lightning Blanket referred to were 1,400

men of the Sixth Minnesota Regiment approaching from St. Paul. They were led by Eagle Chief Henry H. Sibley, also known to the Indians as Long Trader Sibley because he was a trader before he became an Eagle Chief. (Because a colonel's insignia was an eagle, Indians called colonels Eagle Chiefs. Generals were called Star Chiefs.)

At midmorning on August 23, the Santees attacked New Ulm—but the townspeople were ready for this. After the attack on August 19, they had built barricades, brought in more weapons, and secured the help of militia from towns down the valley. Because Little Crow was still too weak from his wounds to fight, Mankato was the war leader. His plan was to surround the town and then attack from all directions at once.

The Siege of New Ulm, Minn. is a 1902 lithograph of a scene from the battle. [LOC, USZC4-2995]

23

The firing on both sides was sharp and rapid. Early in the afternoon, the Santees set fire to several structures on the windward side of New Ulm, intending to advance under a smoke screen. Sixty warriors charged a barricade, but were driven back by heavy volleys. It was a long and bitter battle, fought in the streets, dwellings, outhouses, and store buildings. When darkness fell, the Santees departed without a victory. But they left behind them the smoldering ruins of 190 buildings and more than 100 casualties among the stubborn defenders of New Ulm.

An 1862 photograph taken of white refugees from southwestern Minnesota pausing to eat. They are fleeing the Minnesota River region during Little Crow's War. [LOC, USZ62-29727]

THREE

The Santees Lose Their Homeland

We are only little herds of buffalo left scattered;
the great herds that once covered the prairies are no more.
—LITTLE CROW OF THE SANTEE SIOUX

THREE DAYS AFTER THE BATTLE OF NEW ULM, the first group of troops from Sibley's regiment reached Fort Ridgely. The Santees began withdrawing up the Minnesota Valley. They had taken more than 200 prisoners, mostly white women and children and many half-breeds known to be sympathetic toward the whites. After establishing a temporary village about 40 miles above the Upper Agency, Little Crow began negotiating with other Sioux leaders in the area, hoping to gain their support. He had little success. One reason was Little Crow's failure to drive the soldiers from Fort Ridgely. Another reason was the widespread killing of white settlers on the north side of the Minnesota River by marauding bands of undisciplined young warriors.

Although Little Crow didn't like those attacks on defenseless settlers, he knew his decision to begin the war had unleashed the raiders. It was too late to turn back. The war would go on as long as he had warriors to fight.

On the first day of the Drying Grass Moon (September) in 1862, he decided to scout downriver to test the strength of Sibley's army. The Santees divided into two forces. Little Crow led 110 warriors along the north side of the Minnesota River, while Big Eagle and Mankato searched the south bank with a larger force.

Little Crow's Santees secretly observed activity around the forts at Hutchinson and Forest City, but they discovered little because the soldiers remained within stockades. On September 5, runners brought news of a battle a few miles to the southwest. Big Eagle and Mankato had trapped Sibley's soldiers at Birch Coulee, a place named for the shallow ravine lined with birch trees.

During the night before the battle at Birch Coulee, Big Eagle and Mankato had quietly surrounded the soldiers' camp. The fighting began at dawn and lasted throughout the day. At night the Santees retreated and prepared to renew the attack in the morning.

Big Eagle later remembered that on the morning of the second day

Just as we were about to charge, word came that a large number of mounted soldiers were coming up from the east toward Fort Ridgely. This stopped the charge and created some excitement. Mankato at once took some men from the coulee and went out to meet them. . . . Mankato flourished his men around so, and all the Indians in the coulee kept up a noise, and at last the whites began to fall back, and they

*retreated about two miles and began to dig breastworks [a
protective barrier]. Mankato followed them and left about
thirty men to watch them, and returned to the fight at the
coulee with the rest. The Indians were laughing when they
came back at the way they had deceived the white men, and
we were all glad that the whites had not pushed forward and
driven us away. . . .*

*The next morning General Sibley came with a very large
force and drove us away from the field. We took our time
getting away. Some of our men said they remained till Sibley got up and that they fired at some of his men as they
were shaking hands with some of the men of the camp.
Those of us who were on the prairie went back to the westward and on down the valley. . . . There was no pursuit.*

The warriors set up camp a few miles away at the mouth of
the Chippewa River and were soon joined by Little Crow and
his band. Not long afterward, some warriors discovered a message stuck on an upright pole at the Birch Coulee battlefield. It
was from Long Trader Sibley to Little Crow.

Sibley's message was brief and noncommittal: *If Little Crow
has any proposition to make, let him send a half-breed to me,
and he shall be protected in and out of camp.*

Little Crow did not trust Sibley, who as a trader for the American Fur Company had cheated the Santees. But he decided to
send a reply. He thought that perhaps Sibley did not know why
the Santees had gone to war. Little Crow also wanted Minnesota
governor Alexander Ramsey to know the reasons for the war.

An undated photograph of Governor Alexander Ramsey of Minnesota. He was determined to drive the Sioux out of Minnesota. His policy was backed by almost all the white settlers in the state. *[LOC, DIG-cwpbh-04441]*

Many of the neutrals among the Santees were frightened at what Ramsey had recently told the white Minnesotans: "The Sioux Indians must be exterminated or driven forever beyond the borders of the state."

On September 7, Little Crow wrote,

For what reason we have commenced this war I will tell you. It is on account of Major Galbraith. We made a treaty with the government, and beg for what we do get, and can't get that till our children are dying with hunger. It is the traders who commenced it. Mr. A. J. Myrick told the Indians that they would eat grass or dirt. Then Mr. Forbes told the Lower Sioux that they were not men. Then Roberts [another agent] was working with his friends to defraud us out of our moneys. If the young braves have pushed the white men, I have done this myself. So I want you to let Governor Ramsey know this. I have a great many prisoners, women and children. . . . I want you to give me an answer to the bearer.

Long Trader Sibley's reply was hardly reassuring.

LITTLE CROW—You have murdered many of our people without any sufficient cause. Return me the prisoners under a flag of truce, and I will talk with you then like a man.

Little Crow had no intention of returning the prisoners until he knew whether or not Sibley planned to carry out Governor Ramsey's call to exterminate or exile the Santees. Little Crow wanted to use the prisoners for bargaining. In the councils of the Santees, however, there was much disagreement over what course they should take. Paul Mazakootemane of the Upper Agency Sissetons condemned Little Crow for starting the war. "Give me all these white captives," he demanded. "I will deliver them up to their friends. . . . Stop fighting. No one who fights with the white people ever becomes rich, or remains two days in one place, but is always fleeing and starving."

Wabasha, who had been in the battles at Fort Ridgely and New Ulm, was also in favor of opening a road to peace by freeing the prisoners. But his son-in-law Rda-in-yan-ka spoke for Little Crow and the majority of the warriors in opposing the idea. He said, "I have no confidence that the whites will stand by any agreement they make if we give [the prisoners] up. Ever since we [made a treaty] with them, their agents and traders have robbed and cheated us. Some of our people have been shot, some hung; others placed upon floating ice and drowned; and many have been starved in their prisons." He then talked about the killing incident by the four young warriors that had started the war. "The older ones would have prevented it if they could," he said, "but since the treaties, they have lost all their influence. We may regret what has happened, but the matter has gone too far to be remedied. We have got to die. Let us, then, kill as many of the whites as possible, and let the prisoners die with us."

On September 12, Little Crow sent Sibley another message offering to end the war without further bloodshed. In it he assured Sibley that the prisoners were being treated kindly.

Unknown to Little Crow, on that same day Wabasha sent Sibley a secret message. He blamed Little Crow for starting the war. Wabasha claimed to be a friend of the "good white people." He did not mention that he had fought them at Fort Ridgely and New Ulm. "I have been kept back by threats that I should be killed if I did anything to help the whites," he wrote, "but if you will now appoint some place for me to meet you, myself and the few friends that I have will get all the prisoners we can, and with our family go to whatever place you will appoint for us to meet."

Sibley answered both messages immediately. He scolded Little Crow for not giving up the prisoners, telling him that was not the way to make peace, but he did not answer the war leader's plea for a way to end the fighting. Instead Sibley wrote a long letter to Little Crow's betrayer, Wabasha, giving him instructions for using a truce flag for delivery of the prisoners.

After Little Crow received Sibley's cold reply, he knew there was no hope for peace except total surrender. If the soldiers could not be beaten, then it was either death or exile for the Santee Sioux.

On September 22, scouts reported that Sibley's soldiers had

gone into camp at Wood Lake. Little Crow decided to fight them there. The next morning, just as they had done at Birch Coulee, the Santees silently prepared an ambush for the soldiers. But an accident spoiled their plans.

For some reason, Sibley's men remained in camp. Then sometime around midmorning, a foraging expedition left to dig potatoes at an agency field five miles away. They were on a path headed straight through the warriors' positions. When the troops reached the warriors' line, the Santees stood up and fired.

"The Indians that were in the fight did well, but hundreds of our men did not get into it and did not fire a shot. They were out too far," Big Eagle later said. "The men in the ravine and the line connecting them with those on the road did most of the fighting. Those of us on the hill did our best, but we were soon driven off. Mankato was killed here, and we lost a very good and very brave war chief. He was killed by a cannonball that was so nearly spent that he was not afraid of it, and it struck him in the back as he lay on the ground, and killed him."

That evening in the Santees' camp 12 miles above the Yellow Medicine River, the chiefs held a last council. Most of them were now convinced that Eagle Chief Sibley was too strong for them. The woodland Sioux must surrender or flee to join their cousins, the prairie Sioux of the Dakota country. Those who had taken no part in the fighting decided to stay and surrender, certain that the delivery of the white prisoners would win them the friendship of Sibley forever. They were joined by Wabasha, who persuaded his son-in-law Rda-in-yan-ka to stay. At the last minute, Big Eagle also decided to stay. Rda-in-yan-ka, Big Eagle, and others would soon regret that decision.

Next morning, Little Crow made a last speech to his followers. "I am ashamed to call myself a Sioux," he said. "Seven hundred of our best warriors were whipped yesterday by the whites. Now we had better all run away and scatter out over the plains like buffalo and wolves. To be sure, the whites had wagon-guns and better arms than we, and there were many more of them. But that is no reason why we should not have whipped them, for we are brave Sioux and whites are cowardly women. I cannot account for the disgraceful defeat. It must be the work of traitors in our midst." He, Shakopee, and Medicine Bottle then ordered their people to pack their possessions and head west to the Dakota Territory.

On September 26, with the assistance of Wabasha and Paul Mazakootemane, who displayed truce flags, Sibley marched into the Santee camp, where he demanded and received immediate delivery of the captives. In a council that followed, Sibley announced that the approximately 2,000 Santees there should all consider themselves prisoners of war until he could discover and hang the guilty ones among them. The peace leaders protested, claiming their long-standing friendship.

Sibley replied by surrounding the camp with artillery. He then sent out half-breed messengers to summon all Santees in the Minnesota River Valley to Camp Release (as he had named the place). Those who refused would be hunted down and captured or killed.

Sibley chose five of his officers to form a military court to try all Santees suspected of engaging in the uprising. As the Indians had no legal rights, he saw no reason to appoint a defense lawyer for them.

The first suspect brought before the court was a mulatto named Godfrey, who was married to a woman of Wabasha's band and had been living at the Lower Sioux Agency for four years. Witnesses were three white women who had been among the captives. None accused him of rape, none had seen him commit a murder, but they said they had heard Godfrey boast of killing seven white people at New Ulm. On this evidence the military court found Godfrey guilty of murder and sentenced him to be hanged.

When Godfrey learned that the court would be willing to reduce his death sentence to a prison term if he would identify any Santee guilty of participating in the attacks, he became a willing informant. The trials then proceeded quickly. As many as 40 Indians a day were tried. On the fifth day of the Deer Rutting Moon (November), the trials ended with 303 Santee sentenced to death and 16 to long prison terms.

The responsibility for extinguishing so many human lives was more than Colonel Sibley wanted to bear alone. He asked Brigadier General John Pope, the commander of the Military Department of the Northwest, to authorize the executions.

Brigadier General John Pope, egotistical and unpopular, was exiled to Minnesota and made the commander of the Department of the Northwest after a humiliating defeat by Confederate general Robert E. Lee in the Second Battle of Bull Run. He saw Little Crow's War as a way to restore his reputation. [LOC, DIG-cwpb-06342]

General Pope in turn passed the final decision to the president of the United States, Abraham Lincoln. "The Sioux prisoners will be executed unless the president forbids it," General Pope informed Governor Ramsey, "which I am sure he will not do."

Being a man of conscience, however, Abraham Lincoln asked for "the full and complete record of the convictions; if the record does not fully indicate the more guilty and influential of the culprits, please have a careful statement made on these points and forward to me." On receipt of the trial records, the president assigned two lawyers to examine them to determine who were murderers and who had engaged only in battle.

Lincoln's refusal to authorize the immediate hanging of the condemned Santees angered General Pope and Governor Ramsey. Pope protested that "the criminals condemned ought in every view to be at once executed without exception. . . . Humanity requires an immediate disposition of the case." Ramsey demanded authority from the president to order speedy executions of the 303 condemned men, and warned him that the people of Minnesota would take "private revenge" on the prisoners if Lincoln did not act quickly.

While President Lincoln was reviewing the trial records, Sibley, who had been promoted to general for his victory over the Santees, moved the condemned Indians to a prison camp at South Bend on the Minnesota River. While they were being escorted past New Ulm, a mob of citizens that included many women attempted "private revenge" on the prisoners with pitchforks, scalding water, and hurled stones. Fifteen prisoners were

injured, one with a broken jaw, before the soldiers could march them beyond the town. The Indians were later transferred to a stronger stockade near the town of Mankato.

In the meantime Sibley decided to keep the remaining 1,700 Santee—mostly women and children—as prisoners, although they were accused of no crime other than having been born Indians. He ordered them transferred to Fort Snelling. Along the way they too were assaulted by angry white citizens. At Fort Snelling the four-mile-long procession was shunted into a fenced enclosure on damp lowland by the river. There, under soldier guard, housed in dilapidated shelters, and fed on scanty rations, the remnants of the once proud woodland Sioux awaited their fate.

This 1862 woodcut engraving from Frank Leslie's Illustrated Newspaper *shows Fort Snelling, Minnesota, and troops marching on the plain in front of it.* Frank Leslie's Illustrated Newspaper *was one of the two most popular national publications in America during the 19th century. The other was* Harper's Weekly. *These large (12-by-16-inch) newspapers, with prices ranging from six to ten cents a copy, were famous for their many detailed illustrations.* [LOC, USZ61-2046]

On the sixth day of the Moon When the Deer Shed Their Horns and the Moon of Popping Trees (December), President Lincoln notified Sibley that he should "cause to be executed" 39 of the 303 convicted Santee. "The other condemned prisoners you will hold subject to further orders, taking care that they neither escape nor are subjected to any unlawful violence."

The execution date was December 26. That morning the town of Mankato was filled with vindictive and morbidly curious citizens. A regiment of soldiers marched in to keep order. At the last minute, one Indian was given a reprieve. About ten o'clock, the 38 condemned men were marched from the prison to the scaffold. They sang the Sioux death song until soldiers pulled white caps over their heads and placed nooses around their necks. At a signal from an army officer, the control rope was cut and 38 Santee Sioux dangled lifeless in the air. A spectator boasted that it was "America's greatest mass execution."

A few hours later, officials discovered that two of the men hanged were not on Lincoln's list of approved executions. But nothing was said of the wrongful deaths of the two Santee until nine years afterward. "It was a matter of regret that any mistakes were made," declared one of those responsible. "I feel sure they were not made intentionally." One of the innocent men hanged had saved a white woman's life during the raiding.

Several others who were executed that day had maintained their innocence until the end. One of them was Rda-in-yan-ka. Shortly before his execution, Rda-in-yan-ka dictated a farewell letter to his chief.

A lithograph of the execution in Mankato, Minnesota, on December 26, 1862,
of 38 Sioux warriors convicted for crimes committed during Little Crow's War.
Unusually, this execution was public. It was also the largest execution in
United States history. [LOC, DIG-pga-03790]

Wabasha—You have deceived me. You told me that if we followed the advice of General Sibley, and gave ourselves up to the whites, all would be well; no innocent men would be injured. I have not killed, wounded, or injured a white man, or any white persons. I have not participated in the plunder of their property, and yet today I am set apart for execution, and must die in a few days, while men who are guilty will remain in prison. My wife is your daughter, my children are your grandchildren. I leave them all in your care and under your protection. Do not let them suffer; and when my children are grown up, let them know that their father died because he followed the advice of his chief, and without having the blood of a white man to answer for to the Great Spirit.

My wife and children are dear to me. Let them not grieve for me. Let them remember that the brave should be prepared to meet death, and I will do as becomes a Dakota.

Your son-in-law
Rda-in-yan-ka

Those who escaped execution were sentenced to prison. One of them was Big Eagle. "If I had known that I would be sent to the penitentiary," he later said, "I would not have surrendered." Many of the others also regretted that they had not fled from Minnesota with the warriors.

By the time of the executions, Little Crow and his followers were camped by Devils Lake, a wintering place for several Sioux tribes in the northeast corner of the Dakota Territory. During the winter, he tried to unite the Plains chiefs in a military alliance. He warned them that, unless they were prepared to fight, they would all fall before the invading whites. He won their sympathy, but few of the Plains Indians believed they were in any danger.

In the spring Little Crow, Shakopee, and Medicine Bottle took their bands north into Canada. At Fort Garry (renamed Winnipeg in 1873), Little Crow attempted to persuade the British authorities to aid the Santee. He reminded the British that his grandfather had been their ally in previous wars with the Americans. But the British refused to give the Santee ammunition or weapons. The only help the British would provide was some food and clothing.

In the Strawberry Moon (June) of 1863, Little Crow decided that if he and his family must become Plains Indians, they should have horses. The white men who had driven him from his land had horses; he would take theirs in exchange for the land. He decided to return to Minnesota with a small party to capture horses.

In the Moon of the Red Blooming Lilies (July), Little Crow, his 16-year-old son Wowinapa, 15 warriors, and a squaw reached the Big Woods near Acton Township, where his war had begun. On the afternoon of July 3, Little Crow and Wowinapa left their hidden camping place and went to pick raspberries near the settlement of Hutchinson. About sundown they were sighted by two settlers returning home from a deer hunt. As the state of

Minnesota had recently begun paying $25 in bounty for Sioux scalps, the settlers immediately opened fire.

Little Crow was hit twice. The first musket ball wounded him just above the hip. Wowinapa said the next musket shot was a ricochet that "struck the stock of [Little Crow's] gun, and then hit him in the side, near the shoulder. This was the shot that killed him."

Before the settlers could reach them, Wowinapa hurriedly dressed his dead father in new moccasins for the journey to the Land of Ghosts. He covered the body with a coat and fled to the camp. After warning the other members of the party to scatter, he started back to Devils Lake.

Wowinapa was later captured by some of Sibley's soldiers, who had marched into the Dakota country that summer to kill Sioux. The soldiers returned the 16-year-old boy to Minnesota, where he was given a military trial and sentenced to be hanged. He learned then that his father's scalp and skull had been preserved and placed on exhibition in St. Paul. The state of Minnesota presented the settlers who had killed Little Crow with the regular scalp bounty and a bonus of $500.

When Wowinapa's trial record was sent to Washington, military authorities changed the boy's sentence to imprisonment.

Meanwhile, Shakopee and Medicine Bottle remained in Canada, believing themselves beyond reach of the vengeful Minnesotans. They were wrong.

In December 1863, Major Edwin Hatch and a battalion of

Minnesota cavalry arrived at Pembina in the northeast Dakota Territory, just below the Canadian frontier. From there Hatch sent a lieutenant across the border to Fort Garry to secretly meet with an American citizen, John McKenzie. With the aid of McKenzie and two Canadians, the lieutenant kidnapped Shakopee and Medicine Bottle. In complete disregard of international law, the lieutenant hauled his captives back into the Dakota Territory and delivered them to Major Hatch at Pembina. A few months later, Sibley staged another spectacular trial, and Shakopee and Medicine Bottle were sentenced to be hanged. The St. Paul *Pioneer* newspaper commented about the verdict: "We do not believe that serious injustice will be done by the executions tomorrow, but it would have been more creditable if some tangible evidence of their guilt had been obtained. . . . no white man, tried before a jury of his peers, would be executed upon the testimony thus produced." After the hangings, the Minnesota legislature gratefully appropriated $1,000 as payment to John McKenzie for his services.

The day of the Santee Sioux in Minnesota now came to an end. The uprisings had given the white citizens an opportunity to seize the Santees' remaining lands without even making a show of paying for them. Previous treaties were torn up. The surviving Indians were informed that they would be removed to a reservation in the Dakota Territory. Even those leaders who had collaborated with the white men had to go.

Crow Creek on the Missouri River in the south-central Dakota Territory was the site chosen for the Santee reservation. The soil was barren, rainfall scanty, wild game scarce, and the water unfit for drinking. Soon the surrounding hills were covered with graves. Of the 1,300 Santees brought there in 1863, fewer than 1,000 survived their first winter.

Among the visitors to Crow Creek that year was a young Teton Sioux. He looked with pity upon his Santee cousins and listened to their stories of the Americans who had taken their land and driven them away. He resolved that he would fight to hold the buffalo country of his people. His name was Tatanka Yotanka, the Sitting Bull.

FOUR

War Comes to the Powder River

When the white man comes in my country,
he leaves a trail of blood behind him.
—RED CLOUD OF THE OGLALA SIOUX

IN JULY 1865, unaware that the Civil War had ended four months earlier, the Sioux, Cheyenne, and Arapaho began preparing for their usual summer medicine ceremonies along the Powder River in what is now northeast Wyoming.

By late August, the tribes were scattered from the Bighorn Mountains on the west to the Black Hills on the east. They were so sure that the region was beyond the reach of the Bluecoats that most of them were skeptical when they heard rumors of soldiers coming at them from four directions.

But the rumors were true.

Brigadier General Patrick E. Connor had announced in July that the Indians north of the Platte River "must be hunted like wolves." He organized three columns of soldiers for an invasion of the Powder River country. One column, commanded by Colonel Nelson Cole, would march from Nebraska to the Black Hills of Dakota. A second column, under Colonel Samuel Walker, would move straight north from Fort Laramie to link

Bozeman Trail

Ft. Phil
Kearny

Powder River

Little Powder River

Ft. Reno
(Connor)

WYOMING
TERRITORY

Bighorn
Mountains

BOZEMAN TRAIL

N

W   E

S

North Platte River

Bozeman Trail

Rivers

Mountains

Army forts

Laramie Mountains

Ft. Laramie

Miles

0   25   50

This map of the Powder River basin shows the Bozeman Trail and the two forts, Reno (built in 1865) and Phil Kearny (built in 1866), that were the cause of Red Cloud's War.

up with Cole in the Black Hills. The third column, with Connor himself in command, would head in a northwesterly direction along the Bozeman Trail toward Montana. General Connor thus hoped to trap the Indians between his column and the combined forces of Cole and Walker. He warned his officers to accept no offers of peace from the Indians, and ordered bluntly, "Attack and kill every male Indian over twelve years of age."

In the beginning of August, the three columns set off. If

everything went according to plan, they would rendezvous about September 1 on the Rosebud River in the heart of hostile Indian country.

A fourth group, which had no connection with Connor's plans, was also approaching the Powder River country from the east. Organized by a civilian, James A. Sawyers, to open a new overland route, this expedition had no other objective than to reach the Montana gold fields. Because Sawyers knew he would be trespassing on Indian treaty lands, he expected resistance and therefore had obtained two companies of infantrymen to escort his group of 73 gold seekers and 80 wagons of supplies.

Brigadier General Patrick E. Connor would try to blame subordinates for his failures during the Powder River campaign. [LOC, DIG-cwpb-06318]

It was mid-August when the Sioux and Cheyenne who were camped along the Powder River learned of Sawyers's approaching wagon train. The son of a Cheyenne mother and a white father, George Bent, who chose to live among his mother's people, recalled afterward, "Our village crier, a man named Bull Bear, mounted and rode about our camp, crying that soldiers were coming. . . . Everybody ran for ponies."

About 500 Sioux and Cheyenne were in the war party. Leading the Sioux was an Oglala chief who would become famous for his war against the Bluecoats. His name was Mahpiua-luta, but he was known to the whites as Red Cloud. Leading the Cheyenne was their great chief Tamilapesni,

MAHPÍ-LUTA.   OGLALA LAKOTA.

or Dull Knife. The chiefs were very angry that soldiers had come into their country without asking permission.

When they sighted the wagon train, it was moving along between two hills with a herd of about 300 cattle following behind. The Indians divided and spread out along opposite ridges and, at a signal, began firing upon the soldier escorts. In a few minutes the train formed a circular corral with the cattle herded inside.

For two or three hours, the warriors harassed the soldiers by creeping down gullies and suddenly opening fire at close range. A few of the more daring riders galloped in close, circled the wagons, and then swept out of range. After the soldiers started firing their two howitzers, the warriors kept behind hillocks, uttering war cries and shouting insults.

The wagon train could not move, but neither could the Indians get at it. About midday, to end the stalemate, the chiefs ordered that a white flag be raised.

A meeting was quickly arranged. George Bent and his brother Charlie were the interpreters for Red Cloud and Dull Knife. Colonel Sawyers and Captain George Williford came out with a small escort. (Colonel Sawyers's rank was honorary, but he considered himself in command of the wagon train. Captain Williford's rank was genuine.)

When Red Cloud demanded an explanation for the presence of soldiers in the Indians' country, Captain Williford replied by asking why the Indians had attacked peaceful white men. Sawyers protested that he had not come to fight Indians. He

An undated photograph of Red Cloud in ceremonial dress. Red Cloud is considered one of the greatest American Indian diplomats. [LOC, USZ62-91032]

was seeking a short route to the Montana gold fields and wanted only to pass through the country.

George Bent said afterward, "Red Cloud replied if the whites would go clear out of his country and make no roads it was all right. Dull Knife said the same for the Cheyenne; then both chiefs said for the officer [Williford] to take the [wagon] train due west from this place, then turn north, and when he had passed the Bighorn Mountains, he would be out of their country."

Sawyers again protested. To follow such a route would take him too far out of his way. He said he wanted to move north along the Powder River valley to find a fort that General Connor was building there.

This was the first that Red Cloud and Dull Knife had heard of General Connor and his invasion. They expressed surprise and anger that soldiers would dare build a fort in the heart of their hunting grounds. Seeing that the chiefs were growing hostile, Sawyers quickly offered them a wagonload of goods. Red Cloud suggested that gunpowder and ammunition be added to the list, but Captain Williford objected strongly. In fact, he was opposed to giving the Indians anything.

Finally the chiefs agreed to accept the goods in exchange for granting permission for the wagon train to pass through. After this had been done, the wagon train went on its way. It was later harassed for several days by a second band of Sioux that also demanded goods but was refused.

Meanwhile, Red Cloud and Dull Knife and their warriors

had left to confirm the rumors of soldiers building a fort on the Powder River.

In fact, Star Chief Connor had already started construction of a stockade about sixty miles south of the Crazy Woman Fork and named it in honor of himself, Fort Connor.

On August 22, General Connor decided that the stockade on the Powder River was strong enough to be held by one cavalry company. Leaving most of his supplies there, he led the rest of his men on a forced march, a rapid advance with little rest. They moved northwest toward the Tongue River valley in order to find as quickly as possible any large concentrations of Indian lodges. This group included a number of Pawnee scouts, since the Pawnee were longtime enemies of the Sioux and Arapaho. Had General Connor moved north along the Powder River, he would have found thousands of Red Cloud's and Dull Knife's warriors searching for Connor's soldiers and eager for a fight.

An Edward Curtis photograph taken in 1910 of a young Arapaho woman. [LOC, USZ62-97843]

About a week after Connor's column left the Powder River, a Cheyenne warrior named Little Horse was traveling through this same area with his wife and young son. Little Horse's wife was an Arapaho woman, and they were making a summer visit to see her relatives at Black Bear's Arapaho camp on the Tongue River. One day, a pack on his wife's horse got loose. When she dismounted to tighten it, she happened to

An 1898 Frank A. Rinehart photograph of an Arapaho woman named Freckled Face in ceremonial dress. [LOC, DIG-ppmsca-15854]

glance back across a ridge. A line of mounted men was coming along the trail far behind them.

"Look over there," she called to Little Horse.

"They're soldiers!" Little Horse cried. "Hurry!"

As soon as they were over the next hill and out of view of the soldiers, they turned off the trail. Little Horse cut loose from a packhorse the poles of the travois on which his young son was riding, took the boy on behind him, and they rode fast—straight for Black Bear's camp. They came galloping in, disturbing the peaceful village of 250 lodges pitched on a mesa above the river. The Arapaho were rich in ponies that year. Three thousand were corralled along the stream.

None of the Arapaho believed that soldiers could be within hundreds of miles. When Little Horse's wife tried to get the crier to warn the people, he said, "Little Horse has made a mistake; he just saw some Indians coming over the trail, and nothing more." Certain that the horsemen they had seen were soldiers, Little Horse and his wife hurried to find her relatives. Her brother, Panther, was resting in front of his tepee. They told him that soldiers were coming. "Pack up whatever you wish to take along," Little Horse said. "We must go tonight."

Panther laughed. "You're always getting frightened and making mistakes about things," he said. "You saw nothing but some buffalo."

"Very well," Little Horse replied, "you need not go unless you want to, but we shall go tonight." His wife managed to persuade some of her other relatives, and before nightfall they left the village and moved several miles down the Tongue River.

Meanwhile, some Pawnee scouts under the command of General Connor's subordinate, Captain Frank North, found the Arapaho camp and reported it to Connor. Early the next

A 1908 Edward Curtis photograph of an Atsina Indian on a horse pulling a travois. The Atsinas, also called the Gros Ventre, lived in north-central Montana and were distant neighbors of the Sioux. The travois was the system Plains Indians used to carry their possessions. [LOC, USZ62-97842]

morning, Star Chief Connor's soldiers prepared to attack. By chance, a warrior who had taken one of his racehorses out for a run happened to see the troops assembling behind a ridge. He galloped back to camp as fast as he could and raised a warning.

Moments later, at the sound of a bugle and the blast of a howitzer, 80 Pawnee scouts and 250 of Connor's cavalrymen charged the village from two sides. The village suddenly became a scene of fearsome activity—horses rearing and whinnying, dogs barking, women screaming, children crying, warriors and soldiers yelling and cursing. The Pawnee swerved toward the 3,000 ponies, which the Arapaho herders were desperately trying to scatter along the river valley.

As quickly as they could, the Arapaho mounted ponies and retreated up Wolf Creek, the soldiers chasing them. For 10 miles the Arapaho retreated. When the soldiers' horses tired, the warriors turned on them, shooting their old muskets and bows and arrows. By early afternoon Black Bear and his warriors had pushed Connor's cavalrymen back to the village. But artillerymen had mounted two howitzers there, and the big-talking guns filled the air with whistling pieces of metal, forcing the Arapaho to stop.

While the Arapaho watched from the nearby hills, the soldiers tore down all the lodges in the village. They heaped poles, tepee covers, buffalo robes, blankets, furs, and piles of dried meat called pemmican into great mounds and set fire to them. Everything the Arapaho owned went up in smoke. Then the soldiers and the Pawnee mounted up and went away with 1,000 Arapaho ponies they had captured.

The Arapaho had nothing left except the ponies they had saved from capture, a few old guns, their bows and arrows, and the clothing they were wearing when the soldiers charged into the village. This was the Battle of Tongue River that happened in the Moon When the Geese Shed Their Feathers (August).

Star Chief Connor then marched on toward the Rosebud River, searching for more Indian villages to destroy. As he neared the rendezvous point on the Rosebud, he sent scouts out in all directions to look for the other two columns of his expedition. No trace could be found of either one, and they were a week overdue. On September 9, Connor ordered Captain North to lead his Pawnee mercenaries in a forced march to the Powder River in hopes of intercepting the columns. On the second day the group ran into a blinding sleet storm. Two days later, they found where Cole and Walker had recently camped. The ground was covered with 900 dead horses. Nearby were charred pieces of metal buckles, stirrups, and rings—the remains of saddles and harnesses. Captain North was uncertain what to make of this evidence of a disaster. He immediately turned back to report to General Connor.

Later they learned what had happened.

On August 18 the two columns under Cole and Walker had joined along the Belle Fourche River in the Black Hills. Though the 2,000-man force was strong in numbers, in almost every other respect, it was weak. The soldiers' spirits were low. Before leaving Fort Laramie, the men in one of Walker's regiments mutinied. Only after they were threatened with cannon fire did they agree to march. In addition, the troops had not brought enough food. By late August, rations for the combined columns were so short that they began slaughtering mules for meat. A disease called scurvy broke out among the men. Because of the shortage of grass and water, their horses grew weaker and weaker. With men and horses in such condition, neither Cole nor Walker had any desire to fight Indians. They only wanted to reach the Rosebud River and rendezvous with General Connor.

As for the Indians, most were busy in the sacred places of Paha Sapa, the Black Hills, with their Sun Dances and other religious ceremonies. A few kept watch over the soldiers and reported the Bluecoats' movements. All were angry with the

An Edward Curtis photograph of Cheyennes constructing a Sun Dance lodge in 1910. The Sun Dance is the most important religious ceremony conducted by the Plains Indians and is held during the summer. [LOC, USZ62-106279]

soldiers who trespassed on the sacred soil. But because they were busy with their ceremonies, at first they did not send out any war parties. That soon changed.

On August 28, when Cole and Walker reached the Powder River, they sent scouts to the Tongue and Rosebud rivers to find General Connor, but he was still far to the south. After their scouts returned, the two commanders put their men on half rations and decided to start moving south before starvation brought disaster. What they did not know was that they were being followed. By September 1, nearly 400 Hunkpapa and Minneconjou Sioux warriors were shadowing them. With them was the Hunkpapa leader, Sitting Bull.

When the Sioux war party discovered the soldiers camped in the woods along the Powder, several of the young men wanted to ride in under a truce flag and see if they could persuade the Bluecoats to give them a peace offering. Sitting Bull did not trust white men and was opposed to such begging, but he let the others send a truce party.

The soldiers waited until the Sioux truce party came within easy rifle range and then fired, killing and wounding several before they could escape. On their way back, the survivors made off with several horses from the soldiers' herd.

After looking at the gaunt horses, Sitting Bull decided that 400 Sioux on their fleet-footed mustangs should be an equal match for 2,000 soldiers on such half-starved Army mounts. Most of the other warriors agreed.

Riding down to the camp single file, the Sioux encircled the soldiers guarding the horse herd and began picking them off

This photograph by Orlando Scott Goff shows Sitting Bull in 1881. Goff became famous for his many photographic portraits of Sitting Bull. [LOC, USZ62-12277]

one by one until a company of cavalrymen came charging up the bank of the Powder. The Sioux quickly withdrew on their fast ponies, keeping out of range until the Bluecoats' bony mounts began to falter. Then they turned on their pursuers.

After a few minutes, the soldiers re-formed their ranks, and at the sound of a bugle came charging after the Sioux again. Once more the swift mustangs carried the Sioux warriors out of range. The Indians then scattered, causing the frustrated soldiers to halt. This time the Sioux turned and attacked from all sides. Sitting Bull captured a black stallion.

Alarmed by the Indian attack and fearing worse, the Eagle Chiefs Cole and Walker formed their columns for a forced march southward along the Powder River. For a few days the Sioux followed the soldiers, scaring them by appearing suddenly on ridgetops or making little attacks against the rear guard. Sitting Bull and the other leaders laughed at how frightened the Bluecoats became.

When a big sleet storm struck, the Indians took shelter for two days. At one point they heard scattered firing from the direction of the soldiers' camp. The next day they found the soldiers' abandoned camp. Dead horses were everywhere. The soldiers had shot them because they could not make them go any farther.

Since many of the frightened Bluecoats were now on foot, the Sioux decided to keep following them and drive them so crazy with fear they would never return to the Black Hills. Along the way, these Hunkpapas and Minneconjous began meeting small scouting parties of Oglala Sioux and Cheyennes who were looking for Star Chief Connor's column. There was great excitement in these meetings. Only a few miles south was a large Cheyenne village, and as runners brought the leaders of the bands together, they began planning a big ambush for the soldiers.

The Cheyenne warrior Woqini, known to whites as Roman Nose, was never a chief. But he was regarded by both Indians and whites as one of the greatest warriors of the Plains tribes. Like Red Cloud and Sitting Bull, he was determined to fight for his country. Roman Nose also believed he had powerful protection in battle. It was a warbonnet filled with so many eagle feathers that when he was mounted, the warbonnet trailed almost to the ground. As long as Roman Nose also did not touch anything made by white men or eat anything cooked with white men's utensils before he went into battle, when he wore this warbonnet, the white man's bullets would not touch him.

In September, when the Cheyenne camp first heard about the soldiers fleeing south up the Powder River, Roman Nose asked for the privilege of leading a charge against the Bluecoats. A day or two later, the soldiers were camped in a bend of the river, with high bluffs and thick timber on both sides. Deciding

---

In 1907, Sioux chief High Hawk was photographed in ceremonial dress by Edward Curtis. He is wearing a warbonnet and holding a coup stick. French fur traders gave the coup stick its name. The word coup *is French for "blow" or "strike." For Native Americans, going to war was a major test of manhood. One way a young warrior demonstrated his courage was by "counting coup"—using a coup stick to hit an enemy. This was a highly respected act of bravery because it meant you were close enough to your enemy to risk capture. [LOC, USZ62-48426]*

that this was an excellent place for an attack, the chiefs brought several hundred warriors into position all around the camp. They began the fight by sending small decoy parties in to draw the soldiers out of their wagon corral. But the soldiers would not come out.

Then Roman Nose rode up on his white pony, his warbonnet trailing behind him, his face painted for battle. He called to the Cheyenne warriors not to fight singly as they had always done but to fight together as the soldiers did. The warriors maneuvered their ponies into a line facing the soldiers, who were standing in formation before their wagons. Roman Nose danced his white pony in front of his warriors, telling them to hold fast until he had emptied the soldiers' guns. Then he slapped the pony into a run and rode straight as an arrow toward one end of the line of soldiers. When he was close enough to see their faces clearly, he turned and rode fast along the length of the soldiers' line. They emptied their guns at him all along the way. At the end of the line, he wheeled the white pony and rode back along the soldiers' front again.

"He made three, or perhaps four, rushes from one end of the line to the other," said George Bent, the half-breed Cheyenne. "And then his pony was shot and fell under him. On seeing this, the warriors set up a yell and charged. They attacked the troops all along the line, but could not break through anywhere."

Roman Nose had lost his horse, but his protective medicine saved his life. He also learned some things that day about fighting Bluecoats—and so did Red Cloud, Sitting Bull, Dull Knife, and the other leaders. Bravery, numbers, massive charges—they all meant nothing if the warriors were armed only with bows, lances, clubs, and old trade muskets. The soldiers had modern repeating rifles and the support of howitzers.

For several days after the fight—which would be remembered by the Indians as Roman Nose's Fight—the Cheyenne and Sioux continued to harass the soldiers. The Bluecoats were now barefoot and in rags, and they had nothing left to eat but their bony horses, which they devoured raw because the Indians gave them no time to stop and build fires. At last toward the end of the Drying Grass Moon (September), Star Chief Connor's returning column arrived to rescue Cole's and Walker's beaten soldiers. The soldiers all camped together around the stockade at Fort Connor on the Powder River until messengers from Fort Laramie arrived with orders recalling all troops except for two companies, which were to remain at Fort Connor, renamed Fort Reno in November 1865.

General Connor had left the companies six howitzers to help defend their stockade. Red Cloud and the other leaders studied the fort from a distance. They knew they had enough warriors to storm the stockade, but too many would die under the showers of shot hurled by the big guns. They finally agreed upon a strategy of holding the soldiers prisoners in their fort all winter and cutting off their supplies from Fort Laramie.

Before that winter ended, half the luckless troops in the fort were dead or dying of scurvy, malnutrition, and pneumonia.

Many slipped away and deserted, taking their chances with the Indians outside.

As for the Indians, all except the small bands of warriors needed to watch the fort moved over to the Black Hills, where plentiful herds of antelope and buffalo kept them well fed and comfortable in their warm lodges. Through the long winter evenings, the chiefs recounted the events of Star Chief Connor's invasion. Because the Arapaho had been overconfident and careless, they had lost a village, many lives, and part of their rich pony herd. The other tribes had lost a few lives but no horses or lodges. They had captured horses and mules carrying U.S. brands. They had taken cavalry rifles, saddles, and other equipment from the soldiers. Above all, they had gained a new confidence in their ability to drive the Bluecoat soldiers from their land.

"If white men come into my country again, I will punish them again," Red Cloud said, but he knew that unless he could somehow obtain many new guns like the ones they had captured from the soldiers, and plenty of ammunition for the guns, the Indians could not go on punishing the soldiers forever.

FIVE

Red Cloud's War

I have two mountains in that country—the Black Hills
and the Big Horn Mountain. I want the Great Father to make
no roads through them.

—RED CLOUD OF THE OGLALA SIOUX

WHILE THE INDIANS in the Powder River country were demonstrating their military power, the United States sent a treaty commission to the upper Missouri River. Now that the white man's Civil War was over, the trickle of white immigration to the West was showing signs of increasing to a flood. What the treaty commissioners wanted was right of passageway for trails, roads, and eventually railroads across the Indian country.

At every Sioux village near the river, the commissioners stopped to meet and talk, or parley, about a new treaty with whatever leaders they could find. Newton Edmunds, recently appointed governor of the Dakota Territory, was the prime mover on this commission. Another member was General Henry Sibley, who had driven the Santee Sioux from Minnesota. Edmunds and Sibley handed out blankets, molasses, crackers, and other presents to the Indians they visited and had no difficulty in persuading their hosts to sign new treaties. They also sent runners into the Black Hills and Powder River country inviting the warrior chiefs to come and sign. But the chiefs were busy fighting General Connor's invaders, and none responded.

Before the autumn of 1865 ended, the commissioners had completed nine treaties with the Sioux. Government authorities in Washington proclaimed the end of Indian hostilities. At last the Plains Indians were pacified, they said. Never again would there be a need for expensive campaigns such as Connor's Powder River expedition.

Governor Edmunds and the other commission members knew very well that the treaties were meaningless because not one warrior chief had signed them. Although the commissioners forwarded copies to Washington to be ratified by Congress, they continued their efforts to persuade Red Cloud and the other Powder River chiefs to meet with them at a convenient location for further treaty signings. As the Bozeman Trail was the most important route out of Fort Laramie to Montana, military officials at

Spotted Tail in an undated photograph.
[LOC, USZ62-131515]

the fort were under heavy pressure to persuade Red Cloud and other war leaders to cease their blockade of the Bozeman Trail and siege of Fort Reno, and to come to Laramie at the earliest possible date.

Colonel Henry Maynadier, the commandant at Fort Laramie, tried to find a trustworthy frontiersman to act as intermediary with Red Cloud. But none was willing to go into the Powder River country so soon after Connor had angered the tribes with his invasion. At last Maynadier decided to employ as messengers some Brulé and Oglala chiefs such as Big Mouth, Big Ribs, Eagle Foot, and Whirlwind, who spent much of their time around the fort. Referred to contemptuously as the "Laramie Loafers," these trader Indians were actually shrewd entrepreneurs. If a white man wanted a first-rate buffalo robe at a bargain, or if an Indian up on the Tongue River wanted supplies from the fort commissary, the Laramie Loafers arranged exchanges. They would play an important role as munitions suppliers to the Indians during Red Cloud's war.

During the months of the Moon of Popping Trees (December) and the Moon of Strong Cold (January), Big Mouth and his party spread the news that fine gifts awaited all warrior chiefs if they would come to Fort Laramie and sign new treaties. On January 16, 1866, the messengers returned in company with two bands of Lakota Brulés led by Standing Elk and Swift Bear. The winter had struck these two groups hard. Unable to find enough game and short of shelter, Standing Elk and Swift Bear were eager to sign the treaty and receive clothing and provisions for their cold and hungry people.

"But what about Red Cloud?" Colonel Maynadier wanted to know. "Where were Red Cloud, Man-Afraid-of-His-Horses, Dull Knife—the leaders who had fought Connor's soldiers?" Big Mouth and the other Laramie Loafers assured him that the warrior chiefs would be there in a short time. They could not be hurried, especially in the Moon of Strong Cold.

There was one important Sioux chief who had decided not to join Red Cloud in the war against the Bluecoats. He was the Brulé chief Sinte Gleska, whom the white man called Spotted Tail. Early in the Moon of the Snowblind (March) a messenger arrived from Spotted Tail informing Colonel Maynadier that the Brulé chief was coming to discuss the treaty. Spotted Tail's daughter Fleet Foot was very ill, and he hoped the soldiers' doctor would make her well again. A few days later, when Maynadier heard that Fleet Foot had died en route, he rode out with a company of soldiers and an ambulance to meet the mourning procession of Brulés.

Colonel Maynadier had arranged for a military escort and funeral for Fleet Foot. He hoped that this show of sympathy and respect would help convince Spotted Tail to reopen the Bozeman Trail for the whites. He told Spotted Tail that the Great Father in Washington was sending out a new peace commission in the spring. He wanted Spotted Tail to stay near the fort until the commissioners arrived. It was urgent that the Bozeman Trail be made safe for travel. "I am informed that the travel next spring will be very great," the colonel said, "to the mines of Idaho and Montana."

"We think we have been much wronged," replied Spotted

Tail, "and are entitled to compensation for the damage and distress caused by making so many roads through our country, and driving off and destroying the buffalo and game. My heart is very sad, and I cannot talk on business; I will wait and see the counselors the Great Father will send."

Four days after the funeral for Fleet Foot, Chief Red Cloud, leading a large party of Oglalas, appeared suddenly outside the fort. They stopped first at Spotted Tail's camp, and the two leaders were enjoying a reunion when Maynadier came out with a soldier escort to conduct both of them to his headquarters with the pomp and ceremony of drums and bugles.

When Maynadier told Red Cloud that the new peace

An 1867 Harper's Weekly *wood engraving of train passengers shooting buffalo. This was a popular sport for train passengers, who usually left the dead buffalo to rot.* [LOC, USZ62-cph-3b08935]

commissioners would not arrive at Fort Laramie for some weeks, the Oglala chief became angry. Big Mouth and the other messengers had told him that if he came in and signed a treaty, he would receive presents. He needed guns, ammunition, and provisions. Maynadier replied that he could issue the visiting Oglalas provisions from the army stores, but he had no authority to distribute guns and ammunition. Red Cloud then wanted to know what the treaty would give his people; they had signed treaties before, and it always seemed that the Indians gave to the white men. This time the white men must give something to the Indians.

Remembering that the president of the new commission, E. B. Taylor, was in Omaha, Maynadier suggested that Red Cloud send a message to Taylor over the telegraph wires. Red Cloud was suspicious. He did not entirely trust the magic of the talking wires. After some delay, he agreed to go with the colonel to the fort's telegraph office. Through an interpreter, he dictated a message of peace and friendship to the Great Father's counselor in Omaha.

Commissioner Taylor's reply came clicking back: "The Great Father at Washington . . . wants you all to be his friends and the friends of the white man. If you conclude a treaty of peace, he wishes to make presents to you and your people as a token of his friendship." A trainload of supplies would arrive at Fort Laramie in early June, and he suggested a treaty-signing ceremony be held then.

Red Cloud was impressed. He also liked Colonel Maynadier's straightforward manner. He could wait until the Moon

When the Grass Is Up (June) for the treaty signing. This would give him time to go back to the Powder River and send out runners to all the scattered bands of Sioux, Cheyenne, and Arapaho. It would also give the Indians time to gather more buffalo hides and beaver skins for trading when they came down to Fort Laramie.

As a goodwill gesture, Maynadier issued small amounts of ammunition to the departing Oglalas, and they rode away in fine good humor. Nothing had been said by Maynadier about opening the Bozeman Trail. Nothing had been said by Red Cloud about Fort Reno, the former Fort Connor, which was still under siege on the Powder. These subjects could be postponed until the treaty council.

Red Cloud did not wait for the grass to come up. In 1866, he returned to Fort Laramie in the Moon When the Ponies Shed (May), and he brought with him his chief lieutenant, Man-Afraid-of-His-Horses, and more than 1,000 Oglalas. Dull Knife brought in several lodges of Cheyennes, and a Brulé named Red Leaf arrived with his band. Together with Spotted Tail's people and the other Brulés, they formed a great camp along the Platte River.

A few days later, the peace commissioners arrived, and on June 5 the formal proceedings began, with the usual long orations by commission members and the various Indian leaders. Then Red Cloud unexpectedly asked for a few days' delay while they awaited the arrival of other Tetons who wanted to participate in the discussions. Commissioner Taylor agreed to adjourn the council until June 13.

By a trick of fate, June 13 was the day Colonel Henry B. Carrington and 700 officers and men of the 18th Infantry Regiment reached Fort Laramie. The regiment had marched from Fort Kearney, Nebraska, and was under orders to establish a chain of forts along the Bozeman Trail in preparation for the expected heavy travel to Montana during the summer. Although plans for the expedition had been under way for weeks, none of the Indians invited to attend the treaty signing had been told about this military occupation of the Powder River country.

To avoid friction with the 2,000 Indians camped around Fort Laramie, Carrington halted his regiment four miles east of the post. Standing Elk, one of the Brulé chiefs who had come in during the winter, saw them and rode over to the camp to find out why they were there. After Standing Elk and Carrington had gone through the greeting formalities, Standing Elk asked bluntly, "Where are you going?"

Carrington, known to the Indians as Little White Chief and speaking through his interpreter, replied that he was taking his troops to the Powder River country to guard the road to Montana.

"There is a treaty being made in Laramie with the Sioux that are in the country where you are going," Standing Elk told him. "You will have to fight the Sioux warriors if you go."

Carrington said he was going not to make war on the Sioux but only to guard the still-blockaded Bozeman Trail through the Powder River country.

"They will not sell their hunting grounds to the white men

for a road," Standing Elk insisted. "They will not give you the road unless you whip them." He added quickly that he was a Brulé, that he and Spotted Tail were friends of the white men, but that Red Cloud's Oglalas and the Minneconjous would fight any white men who came north of the Platte.

Before the next day's treaty proceedings, every Indian at Fort Laramie knew why the regiment of Bluecoats was there. When Carrington rode into the fort the next morning, Commissioner Taylor decided to introduce him to the chiefs and quietly inform them of what they already knew—that the United States government intended to open a road through the Powder River country regardless of the treaty.

Carrington's first remarks were

Colonel Henry B. Carrington in a photograph taken between 1860 and 1870. During the Civil War and for a number of years afterward, it was popular for officers to put their right hand inside their uniform jacket, in imitation of French Emperor Napoleon I. [LOC, DIG-cwpb-06857]

drowned out by a chorus of disapproving Indian voices. When he resumed speaking, the Indians continued muttering among themselves and began moving about restlessly. Carrington's interpreter suggested in a whisper that perhaps he should allow the chiefs to speak first.

Man-Afraid-of-His-Horses took the platform. He made it clear that if the soldiers marched into Sioux country, his people would fight them.

Then it was Red Cloud's turn. His lean figure, clad in a light blanket and moccasins, moved to the center of the platform. His straight black hair, parted in the middle, was draped over his shoulders to his waist. His wide mouth was fixed in a determined slit beneath his hawk-like nose. His eyes flashed as he began scolding the peace commissioners for treating the Indians like children. He accused them of pretending to negotiate for a country while they prepared to take it by conquest.

"The white men have crowded the Indians back year by year," he said, "until we are forced to live in a small country north of the Platte, and now our last hunting ground, the home of the People, is to be taken from us. Our women and children will starve, but for my part, I prefer to die fighting rather than by starvation. . . . Great Father sends us presents and wants new road. But [Carrington] goes with soldiers to steal road before Indian says yes or no!"

While the interpreter was still trying to translate the Sioux words into English, the listening Indians became so disorderly that Commissioner Taylor abruptly ended the day's session. Red Cloud strode past Carrington as if he were not there and continued on across the parade ground toward the Oglala camp. Before the next dawn, the Oglalas were gone from Fort Laramie.

SIX

The Fetterman Massacre

It has been our wish to live here in our country peaceably, and do
such things as may be for the welfare and good of our people, but
the Great Father has filled it with soldiers who think only of death.
—SPOTTED TAIL OF THE BRULÉ SIOUX

DURING THE NEXT FEW WEEKS, as Carrington's wagon train moved north along the Bozeman Trail, the Indians had an opportunity to appraise its size and strength. The 200 wagons were loaded with all manner of goods from vegetable seeds to musical instruments for a 25-piece band, as well as the usual military supplies. A number of Bluecoats had also brought their wives and children along, with an assortment of pets and servants.

By June 28, 1866, Carrington's regiment of about 720 men reached Fort Reno, relieving the survivors of the two companies, who were happy to return to Fort Laramie. Carrington left about one-fourth of his regiment, approximately 180 men, to guard Fort Reno and then moved on north, searching for a site for his headquarters post. From Indian camps along the Powder and Tongue rivers, hundreds of warriors now began gathering.

On July 13, the military column halted between the forks of the Little Piney and Big Piney creeks. There in the heart of the best hunting grounds of the Plains Indians, the Bluecoats pitched their army tents and began building Fort Phil Kearny.

Three days later, a large party of Cheyenne arrived. Two Moon, Black Horse, and Dull Knife were among the leaders. Through an interpreter, they sent a message asking if Carrington wanted peace or war. Carrington replied that if they wished to parley, no one would be harmed. A meeting under the flag of truce was arranged, and Carrington allowed 40 chiefs and warriors to enter the fort. What Carrington did not realize was that the meeting was a cover for a secret scouting mission of the fort. The chiefs needed to know how many soldiers there were before they attacked.

A map of Fort Philip Kearney, commonly known as Phil Kearny, Wyoming Territory.

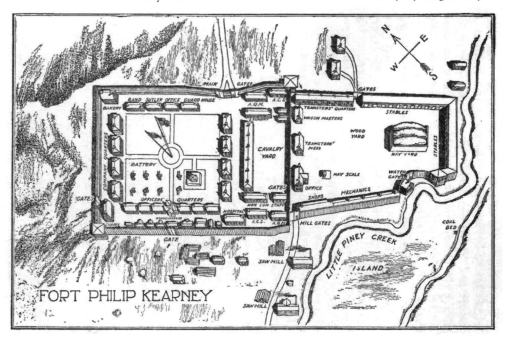

The meeting lasted more than four hours. When it ended, nothing had been decided, though Carrington had learned that there were many more Sioux and Cheyenne warriors in the area than he originally thought. As the Cheyenne prepared to leave, Little White Chief gave them pieces of paper saying that they had agreed to a "lasting peace with the whites and all travelers on the road," and they departed. Within a few hours, villages along the Tongue and Powder rivers heard from the Cheyenne that the new fort was too strong to be captured without great loss. They would have to lure the soldiers out into the open, where they could be more easily attacked.

The next morning at dawn, a band of Red Cloud's Oglalas caused 175 horses and mules from Carrington's herd to stampede. When the soldiers came riding in pursuit, the Indians strung them out in a 15-mile chase and inflicted the first casualties upon Carrington's Bluecoat invaders of the Powder River country.

From that day all through the summer of 1866, Little White Chief Carrington was engaged in a guerrilla war. The Indians' strategy was to make travel on the road difficult and dangerous and to cut off supplies for Carrington's troops, isolate them, and attack. None of the numerous wagon trains, civilian or military, that moved along the Bozeman Trail was safe from surprise attacks. The soldiers soon learned to expect deadly ambushes. Men assigned to cut logs a few miles from Fort Phil Kearny were under constant and deadly harassment.

A 1910 Edward Curtis photograph of Sioux chief Two Moon. [LOC, USZ62-47002]

Red Cloud was everywhere, and his allies increased daily.

Sioux chief Gall, in a photograph taken in 1896.
[LOC, USZ62-117645]

Black Bear, the Arapaho chief whose village had been destroyed by General Connor the previous summer, notified Red Cloud that his warriors were eager to join the fighting. Sorrel Horse, another Arapaho, also brought his warriors into the alliance. Spotted Tail, still believing in peace, had gone to hunt buffalo, but many of his Brulé warriors came north to join Red Cloud. Sitting Bull was there during the summer. Gall, a younger Hunkpapa, was also there. With a Minneconjou known as Hump and a young Oglala warrior named Thasunke Witko, Gall invented clever decoy tricks to taunt, infuriate, and then lure soldiers or settlers into traps. Thasunke Witko would later become more famous than Red Cloud. White men would know him by the name of Crazy Horse. Early in August, Carrington decided that Fort Phil Kearny was strong enough that he could risk dividing his force again. Therefore, in accordance with his instructions from the War Department, he detached 150 men and sent them north 90 miles to build a third fort on the Bozeman Trail—Fort C. F. Smith.

In late summer, Red Cloud had a force of 3,000 warriors. Through their friends the Laramie Loafers, they managed to assemble a small arsenal of rifles and ammunition, but the majority of warriors still had only bows and arrows. During the early autumn, Red Cloud and the other chiefs agreed that they must concentrate their power against Little White Chief and the hated fort on the Pineys. Before the weather turned cold and made travel difficult, they moved toward the Bighorn Mountains and made their camps along the headwaters of the Tongue River in what is now north-central Wyoming. From there they were within easy striking distance of Fort Phil Kearny.

During the summer raiding, two Oglalas—High Back Bone and Yellow Eagle—had made names for themselves with their carefully planned stratagems for tricking the soldiers, as well as for reckless horsemanship and daring hand-to-hand attacks after the soldiers fell into their traps. High Back Bone and Yellow Eagle sometimes worked with young Crazy Horse in planning their elaborate decoys. Early in the Moon of Popping Trees (December), they began taunting the woodcutters in the pine forest near Fort Phil Kearny and the soldiers guarding the wagons that brought wood to the fort.

On December 6, when cold air flowed down the slopes of the Bighorns, High Back Bone and Yellow Eagle took about 100 warriors and dispersed them at various points along the road that connected the pine forest to the fort. Red Cloud was with another group of warriors who took positions along the ridgetops. They flashed mirrors and waved flags to signal the movements of the troops to High Back Bone and his decoys.

Before the day was over, the Indians had the Bluecoats dashing about in all directions. At one time Little White Chief Carrington came out and gave chase. Choosing just the right moment, Crazy Horse dismounted and showed himself on the trail in front of one of Carrington's hot-blooded young cavalry officers, who immediately led a file of soldiers galloping in pursuit. As soon as the soldiers were strung out along the narrow trail, Yellow Eagle and his warriors sprang from concealment behind them. In a matter of seconds, the Indians swarmed over the soldiers.

In their camps that night and for several days following, the chiefs and warriors talked of how foolishly the Bluecoats had acted. Red Cloud was sure that if they could entice a large number of troops out of the fort, a thousand Indians armed with only bows and arrows could kill them all. The chiefs agreed that after the next full moon they would prepare a great trap for Little White Chief and his soldiers.

By the third week of December, everything was in readiness, and about 2,000 warriors began moving south along the Tongue River. The weather was very cold. Most of them rode packhorses, leading their fast-footed war ponies by ropes. Some had rifles, but most were armed with bows and arrows, knives, and lances.

About 10 miles north of Fort Phil Kearny, the Sioux, Cheyenne, and Arapaho made a temporary camp. Between the camp and the fort was the place selected for the ambush—the little valley of Peno Creek.

On the morning of December 21, the chiefs and medicine

men decided the day was favorable for a victory. In the first gray light of dawn, a party of warriors started off in a wide circuit toward Wood Cutter's Road, where they were to make a fake attack against the wagons. Ten young men had already been chosen for the dangerous duty of decoying the soldiers— two Cheyenne, two Arapaho, and two from each of the three Sioux divisions, Oglala, Minneconjou, and Brulé. Crazy Horse, Hump, and the Cheyenne Little Wolf were the leaders. While the decoys mounted and started off toward Lodge Trail Ridge, the main body of warriors moved down the Bozeman Trail. Patches of snow and ice lay along the shady sides of the ridges, but the day was bright, the air cold and dry. About three miles from the fort, where the road ran along a narrow ridge and descended to Peno Creek, they began laying a great ambush. The Cheyenne and Arapaho took the west side. Some of the Sioux hid in a grassy flat on the opposite side; others remained mounted and concealed themselves behind two rocky ridges. By midmorning almost 2,000 warriors were waiting there for the decoys to bring the Bluecoats into the trap.

While the war party was making its fake attack against the wagon train, which was loaded with freshly cut wood, Crazy Horse and the decoys dismounted and hid on a slope facing the fort. At the first sound of gunfire, a company of soldiers dashed out of the fort and galloped off to rescue the woodcutters. As soon as the Bluecoats were out of sight, the decoys showed themselves on the slope and moved closer to the fort. Crazy Horse waved his red blanket and darted in and out of the brush that fringed the frozen Little Piney Creek. After a few minutes

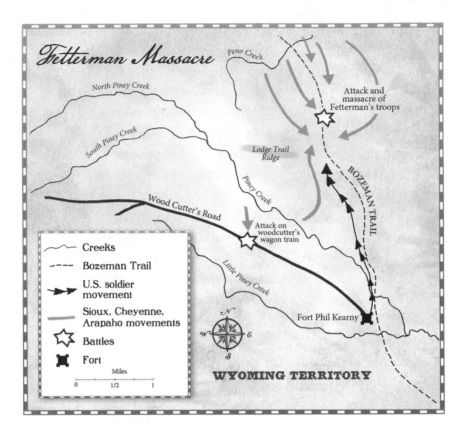

This map of the Fetterman Massacre shows the movement of troops and warriors and where Captain Fetterman's force was wiped out.

of this, Carrington in the fort fired off his big twice-shooting gun. The decoys scattered along the slope, jumping, zigzagging, and yelling to make the soldiers believe they were frightened. By this time the war party had withdrawn from the woodcutters' wagon train and doubled back toward Lodge Trail Ridge. In a few minutes, a mixed cavalry and infantry command led by Captain William J. Fetterman arrived. Fetterman had orders not to pursue the warriors beyond Lodge Trail Ridge.

Crazy Horse and the other decoys jumped on their ponies and began riding back and forth along Lodge Trail Ridge,

taunting the soldiers and angering them so that they fired recklessly. Bullets ricocheted off the rocks, and the decoys moved
back slowly. Whenever the cavalry slowed its advance or halted
to allow the infantry to catch up, Crazy Horse would dismount
and pretend to adjust his pony's bridle or examine its hooves.
The soldiers had seen such tricks in the past. But Crazy Horse
was such a skillful actor that this time the soldiers thought he
was really having problems. Anxious to kill or capture Crazy
Horse and the other decoys, the cavalry rushed forward, shooting wildly. But Crazy Horse and the others managed to keep
just out of range as the Bluecoats entered the Peno Creek valley.
The soldiers shouted with satisfaction. Because the creek was
bordered on both sides by high ridges, they thought the Indians
were trapped. The cavalry spurred their horses on. The infantrymen followed as fast as they could on foot.

But once both groups of soldiers, totaling 81 men, reached
the valley, they realized they were the ones who had fallen into
a trap. As soon as the decoys saw this, they divided into two
parties and quickly rode across each other's trail. This was the
signal for the warriors to attack.

Both cavalry and infantry were stunned to find themselves
suddenly surrounded by warriors. The infantrymen were
quickly killed, but the cavalrymen retreated to a rocky height
near the end of a ridge. They turned their horses loose and
tried to take cover among the ice-encrusted boulders.

Toward the end of the fighting, the Cheyenne and Arapaho
on one side and the Sioux on the other were so close that they
began hitting each other with their showers of arrows. Then it

was all over. Not a soldier was left alive. This was the fight the white men called the Fetterman Massacre. The Indians called it the Battle of the Hundred Slain.

Two weeks later, the Moon of Strong Cold (January) began. There would be no more fighting for a while. The soldiers who were left alive in the fort would have a bitter taste of defeat in their mouths. If they had not learned their lesson and were still there when the grass greened in the spring, the war would continue.

An 1867 Harper's Weekly *woodcut illustrating a scene from the Fetterman Massacre on December 21, 1866. [LOC, USZ62-130184]*

SEVEN

A Treaty Is Signed

*When people come to trouble, it is better for both parties to
come together without arms and talk it over and find some
peaceful way to settle it.*

—SPOTTED TAIL OF THE BRULÉ SIOUX

THE FETTERMAN MASSACRE made a profound impression
upon the United States government. It was the worst defeat the army had yet suffered in Indian warfare. Carrington
was recalled from command, reinforcements were sent to the
forts in the Powder River country, and a new peace commission was dispatched from Washington to Fort Laramie in
1867.

The new commission was headed by John Sanborn, an expe-
rienced negotiator with Indians and known to them as Black
Whiskers. Sanborn and General Alfred Sully arrived at Fort
Laramie in the Geese Laying Moon (April). Their mission was
to persuade Red Cloud and the Sioux to give up their hunting
grounds on the Powder River country and live on a reservation.
As in the previous year, the Brulés were the first to arrive—
Spotted Tail, Swift Bear, Standing Elk, and Iron Shell.

Little Wound and Pawnee Killer, Oglala leaders who had
brought their bands down to the Platte River in hopes of find-
ing buffalo, came to see what gifts the commissioners might be

handing out. Man-Afraid-of-His-Horses arrived as a representative for Red Cloud. When the commissioners asked him if Red Cloud was coming to talk peace, Man-Afraid-of-His-Horses replied that the Oglala leader would not talk about peace until all soldiers were removed from the Powder River country.

A steam locomotive. [LOC, DIG-stereo-1s00612]

During these parleys, Sanborn asked Spotted Tail to address the assembled Indians. Spotted Tail advised his listeners to abandon warfare with the white men and live in peace and happiness. For this, he and the Brulés received enough ammunition to go on a buffalo hunt. The hostile Oglalas received nothing. Man-Afraid-of-His-Horses returned to join Red Cloud, who had already resumed raiding along the Bozeman Trail. Little Wound and Pawnee Killer followed the Brulés to the buffalo ranges. Black Whiskers Sanborn's peace commission had accomplished nothing.

In their search for buffalo and antelope, the Oglalas and Cheyenne crossed railroad tracks several times that summer. Sometimes they saw Iron Horses (locomotives) dragging wooden houses on wheels at great speed along the tracks. They puzzled over what could be inside the houses, and one day a Cheyenne decided to rope one of the Iron Horses and pull it

An 1867 Harper's Weekly *woodcut illustrating an attack by Cheyenne warriors on a work crew building a railroad track. Though war parties repeatedly attacked railroad work crews, they were unable to stop the construction of railroad lines through their land. [LOC, USZ62-115324]*

from the tracks. Instead, the Iron Horse jerked him off his pony and dragged him unmercifully before he could get loose.

One of the warriors in the group, Sleeping Rabbit, suggested they try another way to catch one of the Iron Horses. "If we could bend the track up and spread it out, the Iron Horse might fall off," he said. "Then we could see what is in the wooden houses on wheels." They did this and waited for the train. Eventually one arrived and, as Sleeping Rabbit said, once the locomotive ran over the section where the rails had been removed, it tumbled over onto its side. Huge clouds of smoke and steam poured out of the wrecked locomotive. Men came running from the train, and the Indians killed all but two, who escaped. Then the Indians broke open the houses on wheels and found sacks of flour, sugar, and coffee; boxes of shoes; and other items. After a while the Indians took hot coals from the wrecked engine and set the boxcars on fire. Then they rode away.

Incidents such as this, together with Red Cloud's continuing

war, brought travel by settlers and other civilians to an end through the Powder River country. The government was determined to protect the route of the Union Pacific Railroad. But even the chief army general William Tecumseh Sherman, called Great Warrior Sherman by the Indians, was beginning to wonder if it might not be advisable to leave the Powder River country to the Indians in exchange for peace along the Platte Valley.

Late in July 1867, after holding their Sun Dances and medicine-arrow religious ceremonies, the Sioux and Cheyenne decided to wipe out one of the forts on the Bozeman Trail. Red Cloud wanted to attack Fort Phil Kearny, but Dull Knife and Two Moon thought it would be easier to take Fort C. F. Smith because Cheyenne warriors had already killed or captured nearly all the soldiers' horses there. Finally, after the chiefs could reach no agreement, the Sioux said they would attack Fort Phil Kearny, and the Cheyenne went north to Fort C. F. Smith.

On August 1, some 500 or 600 Cheyenne warriors caught 30 soldiers and civilians in a hayfield about two miles from Fort C. F. Smith. The defenders were armed with new Springfield repeating rifles, which the Cheyenne had not yet seen. When the warriors charged the soldiers' log corral, they met such a heavy barrage of rifle fire that only one warrior was able to penetrate the fortifications, and he was killed. The Cheyenne then set ablaze the high dry grass around the corral.

This was enough for the Cheyenne that day. Many warriors sustained bad wounds from the rapidly firing guns, and about 20 were dead. They started back south to see if the Sioux had had any better luck at Fort Phil Kearny.

The Sioux had not. After making several fake attacks around the fort, Red Cloud decided to use the decoy trick that had worked so well with Captain Fetterman. Crazy Horse would attack the woodcutters' camp, and when the soldiers came out of the fort, High Back Bone would swarm down on them with 800 warriors. Crazy Horse and his decoys carried out their assignment perfectly, but for some reason, several hundred warriors rushed out of concealment too soon, warning the soldiers of their presence.

To salvage something from the fight, Red Cloud turned the attack against the woodcutters, who had taken cover behind a corral of 14 wagon beds reinforced with logs. Several hundred mounted warriors made a circling approach, but these defenders were also armed with Springfields. Faced with rapid and continuous fire from the new weapons, the Sioux quickly pulled their ponies out of range.

The Indians considered neither the Hayfield nor the Wagon Box battles, as they were later called, a defeat. Although some soldiers may have thought of the fights as victories, the United States government did not. Only a few weeks later, General Sherman himself was traveling westward with a new peace council. This time the military authorities were determined to end Red Cloud's war by any means short of surrender.

In the late summer of 1867, Spotted Tail received a message from Nathaniel Taylor, the commissioner responsible for negotiating a treaty with the warring tribes. The Brulés had been roaming peacefully below the Platte, and the commissioner asked Spotted Tail to inform as many Plains chiefs as possible that ammunition would be issued to all friendly Indians sometime during the Drying Grass Moon (September). The chiefs were to assemble at the end of the Union Pacific Railroad track, which was then in western Nebraska. Great Warrior Sherman and six new peace commissioners would come there on the Iron Horse to parley with the chiefs and discuss how to end Red Cloud's war.

Spotted Tail sent for Red Cloud, but the Oglala chief again declined, sending Man-Afraid-of-His-Horses to represent him. Though not a chief, the respected Oglala warrior Pawnee Killer agreed to go. The Cheyenne chief Turkey Leg said he would attend. The two Brulé chiefs, Swift Bear and Standing Elk, as well as Big Mouth and other Laramie Loafers also made the trip. Several other Brulé chiefs responded to the invitation as well.

On September 19, a shiny railroad car arrived at Platte City station, and Great Warrior Sherman, Commissioner Taylor, Major General William S. Harney, known to the Indians as White Whiskers Harney, Black Whiskers Sanborn, and others stepped out.

Commissioner Taylor began the proceedings. "We are sent out here to inquire and find out what has been the trouble. We want to hear from your own lips your grievances and complaints. My friends, speak fully, speak freely, and speak the whole truth. . . . War is bad, peace is good. We must choose the good and not the bad. . . . I await what you have to say."

Spotted Tail replied, "The Great Father has made roads stretching east and west. Those roads are the cause of all our troubles. . . . The country where we live is overrun by whites. All our game is gone. This is the cause of great trouble. I have been a friend of the whites, and am now. . . . If you stop your roads, we can get our game. That Powder River country belongs to the Sioux. . . . My friends, help us; take pity on us."

On the following day, Sherman addressed the chiefs, blandly assuring them that he had thought of their words all night and was ready to give a reply. "The Powder River road was built to furnish our men with provisions," he said. "The Great Father thought that you consented to give permission for that road at Laramie last spring, but it seems that some of the Indians were not there and have gone to war."

Subdued laughter from the chiefs may have surprised Sherman, but he went on, his voice taking a harsher tone. "While the Indians continue to make war upon the road, it will not be given up. But if, on examination, at Laramie in November, we find that the road hurts you, we will give it up or pay for it. If you have any claims, present them to us at Laramie."

Sherman launched into a discussion of the Indians' need for land of their own, advised them to give up their dependence upon wild game, and then he dropped a thunderbolt: "We therefore propose to let the whole Sioux nation select their country up the Missouri River, embracing the White Earth and Cheyenne rivers, to have their lands like the white people, forever, and we propose to keep all white men away except such agents and traders as you may choose."

As these words were translated, the Indians expressed surprise. So this was what the new commissioners wanted them to do—pack up and move far away to the Missouri River! For years the Teton Sioux had been following wild game westward; why should they go back to the Missouri to starve? Why could they not live in peace where game could still be found? Had the greedy eyes of the white men already chosen these bountiful lands for their own?

During the remainder of the discussions, the Indians were uneasy. Swift Bear and Pawnee Killer made friendly speeches in which they asked for ammunition, but the meeting ended in an uproar when Great Warrior Sherman proposed that only the Brulés should receive ammunition. When Commissioner Taylor and White Whiskers Harney pointed out that all the chiefs had been invited to the council with the promise of hunting ammunition, Sherman withdrew his opposition, and small amounts of ammunition were given to the Indians.

Man-Afraid-of-His-Horses wasted no time in returning to Red Cloud's camp on the Powder River. If Red Cloud had had any intention of meeting the new peace commissioners at Laramie during the Moon of Falling Leaves (November), he changed his mind after hearing his representative's report.

On November 9, when the commissioners arrived at Fort

General William Tecumseh Sherman, commander in chief of the U.S. Army during the Sioux wars. Sherman was born and raised in Ohio, not far from where the Shawnee chief Tecumseh was born. Sherman's father was a great admirer of Tecumseh and, out of respect for the Shawnee leader, made Tecumseh his son's middle name. [LOC, DIG-cwpbh-00593]

Laramie, they found only a few Crow chiefs waiting to meet with them. The Crows were friendly, but one of them—Bear Tooth—made a surprising speech in which he condemned all white men for their reckless destruction of wildlife and the natural environment:

Nature's Cattle, *an 1899 illustration of buffalo and antelope by Charles M. Russell. Millions of buffalo roamed the prairie for centuries. Between 1868 and 1881, white hunters killed about 31 million. By 1890, buffalo were almost extinct.* [LOC, USZ62-115203]

Fathers, your young men have devastated the country and killed my animals, the elk, the deer, the antelope, my buffalo. They do not kill them to eat them; they leave them to rot where they fall. Fathers, if I went into your country to kill your animals, what would you say? Should I not be wrong, and would you not make war on me?

COPYRIGHTED BY

A few days after the commissioners' meeting with the Crows, messengers arrived from Red Cloud. He would come to Laramie to talk peace, he informed the commissioners, as soon as the soldiers withdrew from the forts on the Powder River road. The war, he repeated, was being fought for one purpose—to save the valley of the Powder, the only hunting ground left his nation, from intrusion by white men.

For the third time in two years, a peace commission had failed. Before the commissioners returned to Washington, however, they sent Red Cloud a shipment of goods with another plea to come to Laramie as soon as the winter snows melted in the spring. Red Cloud politely replied that he had received the peace offering and that he would come to Laramie as soon as the soldiers left his country.

In the spring of 1868, Great Warrior Sherman and the same peace commission returned to Fort Laramie. This time they had firm orders from an impatient government to abandon the forts on the Powder River road and obtain a peace treaty with Red Cloud. This time they sent a special agent from the Office of Indian Affairs to personally invite the Oglala leader to a peace signing. Red Cloud told the agent he would need about 10 days to consult with his allies and would probably come to Laramie during May, the Moon When the Ponies Shed.

Only a few days after the agent returned to Laramie, however, a message arrived from Red Cloud: "We are on the mountains looking down on the soldiers and the forts. When we see the soldiers moving away and the forts abandoned, then I will come down and talk."

This was all very humiliating to Great Warrior Sherman and the commissioners. They managed to obtain the signatures of a few minor chiefs who came in for presents, but as the days passed, the frustrated commissioners quietly departed one by one for the East. By late spring, only Black Whiskers Sanborn and White Whiskers Harney were left to negotiate. Red Cloud and his allies remained on the Powder through the summer, keeping a close watch on the forts and the road to Montana.

At last the reluctant War Department issued orders for the abandonment of the Powder River forts. On July 29, the troops at Fort C. F. Smith packed their gear and started marching southward. Early the next morning, Red Cloud led a band of celebrating warriors into the post, and they set fire to every building. Fort Phil Kearny was abandoned a month later, and the honor of burning it was given to the Cheyenne under Little Wolf. A few days after that, the last soldier departed from Fort Reno, and the Powder River road was officially closed.

After two years of resistance, Red Cloud had won his war. For a few more weeks, he kept the treaty makers waiting, and then on November 6, surrounded by an escort of triumphant warriors, he came riding into Fort Laramie. Now a conquering hero, he would sign the treaty: "From this day forward all war between the parties to this agreement shall forever cease. The government of the United States desires peace, and its honor is hereby pledged to keep it. The Indians desire peace, and they now pledge their honor to maintain it."

That peace, and the respect for Sioux and Cheyenne land, would last only four years.

EIGHT

Breaking the Treaty of Fort Laramie

These promises have not been kept. . . .
All the words have proved to be false.
—SPOTTED TAIL OF THE BRULÉ SIOUX

IN THE SIOUX TREATY OF 1868, also known as the Treaty of Fort Laramie (1868) to distinguish it from another treaty signed at Fort Laramie in 1851, the United States government set aside the following land for the Sioux: most of Dakota Territory south and west of the Missouri River, the Powder River country of eastern Wyoming Territory and southeastern Montana Territory, and a large section of northwest Nebraska. This land was basically divided into two types: open wilderness, which included *Paha Sapa*, the Black Hills, and reservations or agencies, which were scattered throughout the treaty land. The largest of these was called the Great Sioux Reservation. Smaller reservations were created for chiefs who had signed the treaty. Red Cloud and Spotted Tail were each given reservations in northwestern Nebraska. Other reservations were located along the western bank of the Missouri River.

According to the treaty, all Sioux who agreed to live on reservations in this area would receive money and supplies from

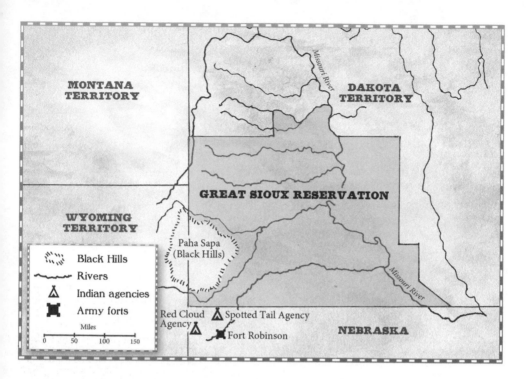

MONTANA TERRITORY

DAKOTA TERRITORY

Missouri River

WYOMING TERRITORY

GREAT SIOUX RESERVATION

Paha Sapa
(Black Hills)

Missouri River

Black Hills
Rivers
Indian agencies
Army forts

Miles
0   50   100   150

Red Cloud
Agency

Spotted Tail Agency

Fort Robinson

NEBRASKA

Before it was later divided into smaller reservations, the Great Sioux Reservation occupied what is now the western half of South Dakota and the southwestern quarter of North Dakota.

the government on a regular basis. They would also be given instructors and receive other assistance to help them learn the ways of the white man. Deciding whether to move to the reservations or not was difficult for the Sioux peoples. They knew it meant abandoning their traditional way of life. Red Cloud, Spotted Tail, and other older chiefs saw that the only way for their people to survive was to move to the reservation. But younger chiefs who had not signed the treaty, including Sitting Bull and Crazy Horse, rejected reservation life and chose to live and hunt in the wilderness areas. The rebellious independence of Sitting Bull and Crazy Horse made them heroes among the young warriors who had followed their parents to the reservation. They resented the way the white men were treating them. It was only a matter of time until that resentment led to another war.

Not long after Red Cloud and Spotted Tail and their people settled on their reservations, rumors began to fly among the white settlements that immense amounts of gold were hidden in Paha Sapa, the Black Hills.

Paha Sapa was the center of the world for the Sioux, the place of gods and holy mountains, where warriors went to speak with the Great Spirit and await visions. In the 1868 treaty, the

This 1875 Harper's Weekly *woodcut illustration shows agents at Red Cloud's reservation distributing rations and goods to the Sioux. [LOC, USZ62-38020]*

United States gave the Sioux the Black Hills forever and made it forbidden for white men to trespass. But four years after the treaty had been signed, white miners were violating the treaty, searching the rocky passes and clear streams of Paha Sapa for the yellow metal that drove white men crazy. When Indians found these crazy white men in their sacred hills, they killed them or chased them out. By 1874 there was such a mad clamor from gold-hungry Americans that the army was ordered to explore the Black Hills. The United States government did not bother to obtain consent from the Indians before starting on this invasion, although the treaty of 1868 prohibited white men from entering without the Indians' permission.

During the Moon of the Red Cherries (July), more than 1,000 mounted soldiers marched across the Plains from Fort Abraham Lincoln to the Black Hills. They were the Seventh Cavalry, and at their head rode Lieutenant Colonel George Armstrong Custer. The Sioux called him Pahuska, or Long Hair.

When Red Cloud heard about Long Hair's expedition, he and the chiefs of the Cheyenne, Arapaho, and other Sioux tribes protested. The anger of the Indians was strong enough that the Great Father, President Ulysses S. Grant, announced his determination "to prevent all invasion of this country by intruders so long as by law and treaty it is secured to the Indians."

But when Custer reported that the hills were filled with gold "from the grass roots down," parties of white men began forming like summer locusts, crazy to begin panning and digging.

George Armstrong Custer in a photo taken in 1865, when he was about 25 years old.
[LOC, DIG-cwpgb-05341]

The trail that Custer's supply wagons had cut into the heart of Paha Sapa soon became known as the Thieves' Road.

In the autumn following Custer's expedition, the Sioux who had been hunting in the north began returning to the Red Cloud agency. They were angry as hornets over the invasion of Paha Sapa. Some talked of forming a war party to go after the miners who were pouring into the hills. Red Cloud listened to the talk, but advised the young men to be patient. He was sure the Great Father would keep his promise and send soldiers to drive out the miners. Though still angry, the young warriors calmed down. Then in October, J. J. Saville, the government agent at Red Cloud's reservation, did something foolish that wrecked Red Cloud's diplomacy and caused the young warriors to reject the old chief's leadership.

Red Cloud and his followers had settled near Camp Robinson (in 1878 it would be named Fort Robinson) in the far northwest corner of Nebraska, about 20 miles south of the Dakota Territory border. In addition to the soldiers' fort, the government had constructed a number of homes and buildings close to Red Cloud's settlement, including an agency warehouse used to store supplies and goods for Red Cloud's people. This warehouse, along with some other government buildings, was surrounded by a stockade. Saville told some white workers to begin setting up a flagpole so that the United States flag could fly over the stockade. The Indians protested. Long Hair Custer had flown flags in his camps across the Black Hills; they wanted no flags or anything else in their agency to remind them of soldiers. Saville ignored the protests. When workers started digging a hole for the flagpole, a band of young warriors came with axes and began chopping the pole to pieces. Saville ordered them to stop, but they paid no attention. The agent went to Red Cloud's office nearby and begged him to stop the warriors. Red Cloud refused.

Furious, Saville brought in cavalry troops. Tensions quickly rose, and though some warriors tried to burn down the stockade, the older chiefs Red Dog and Man-Afraid-of-His-Horses (now known as Old-Man-Afraid-of-His-Horses because his son had taken the name Young-Man-Afraid-of-His-Horses) managed to end the demonstration before anyone was hurt or killed.

Through it all, Red Cloud refused to interfere. He was not surprised when many of the protesters packed up their tepees and belongings and started back north to spend the winter off the reservation. They had proved to him that there were still Sioux warriors who would never take lightly any invasion of Paha Sapa. But Red Cloud did not realize that his authority as a chief was now in decline. In the future, younger warriors would look to Sitting Bull and Crazy Horse, neither of whom had ever lived on a reservation or taken the white man's handouts, for leadership.

By the spring of 1875, tales of Black Hills gold had brought hundreds of miners into Paha Sapa. The army sent soldiers to stop the flow of prospectors. A few were removed from the hills, but no legal action was taken against them, and they soon returned to prospect their claims.

Alarmed by the white men's gold craze and the army's

failure to protect their territory, Red Cloud and Spotted Tail made strong protests to Washington officials. The Great Father's response was to send out a commission to make a treaty with the Sioux "for the relinquishment of the Black Hills." In other words, the time had come to take away one more piece of terri-

Brigadier General Alfred H. Terry, whose name among the Sioux was One Star Terry.
[LOC, DIG-cwpbh-00101]

tory that had been assigned to the Indians in perpetuity. As usual, the commission was made up of politicians, missionaries, traders, and military officers. Senator William B. Allison of Iowa was the chairman. Reverend Samuel D. Hinman was the principal missionary. Brigadier General Alfred Terry—known to the Indians as One Star Terry—represented the military. John Collins, post trader at Fort Laramie, represented the commercial interests.

To ensure representation of nonagency as well as agency Indians, runners were sent to invite Sitting Bull, Crazy Horse, and other "wild" chiefs to the council. A half-breed named Louis Richard took the government letter to Sitting Bull and read it to him.

"I want you to go and tell the Great Father," Sitting Bull responded, "that I do not want to sell any land to the government."

He picked up a pinch of dust

and added, "Not even as much as this." Crazy Horse was also opposed to the selling of Sioux land, especially the Black Hills. He refused to attend the council, but he sent his lieutenant Little Big Man to be an observer for the free Oglalas.

If the commissioners expected to meet quietly with a few compliant chiefs and arrange an inexpensive trade, they were in for a rude surprise. When they arrived at the meeting place, the plains for miles around were covered with Sioux camps and immense herds of grazing ponies. Representatives from all the Sioux nations and many of their Cheyenne and Arapaho friends—more than 20,000 Indians—had gathered.

Few of them had seen a copy of the treaty of 1868, but many knew the meaning of a certain clause in that sacred document: "No treaty for the cession of any portion or part of the reservation herein described . . . shall be of any validity or force . . . unless executed and signed by at least three-fourths of all the adult male Indians occupying or interested in the same." Even if the commissioners had been able to intimidate or to buy off every chief present, they could not have obtained more than a few dozen signatures from the thousands of angry, well-armed warriors determined to keep every pinch of dust and blade of grass within their territory.

On September 20, 1875, the commission assembled under the shade of a large tarp. The commissioners seated themselves on chairs facing the thousands of Indians who were moving restlessly about in the distance. A troop of 120 cavalrymen on white horses filed in from Camp Robinson, as it was then

A 1904 caricature of Senator William B. Allison. [LOC, USZ62-98134]

known, and drew up in a line behind the canvas shelter. Spotted Tail arrived in a wagon from his agency, but Red Cloud had announced that he would not be there. A few other chiefs drifted in, and then suddenly a cloud of dust boiled up from the crest of a distant rise. A band of Indians came galloping down upon the council shelter. The warriors were dressed for battle, and as they came nearer they swerved to encircle the commissioners, fired their rifles skyward, and gave out a few whoops before trotting off to form a line immediately to the rear of the cavalrymen. By this time, a second band of Indians was approaching, and thus, tribe by tribe, the Sioux warriors came in, making their demonstrations of power, until a great circle of several thousand Indians enclosed the council. Now the chiefs came forward, well satisfied that they had given the commissioners something strong to think about. They sat in a semicircle facing the nervous white men, eager to hear what they would have to say about the Black Hills.

A few days earlier, the commissioners had been at Camp Robinson observing the mood of the Indians. They recognized the futility of trying to buy the hills and had decided instead to negotiate for the mineral rights. "We have now to ask you if you are willing to give our people the right to mine in the Black Hills," Senator Allison began, "as long as gold or other valuable minerals are found, for a fair and just sum. If you are so willing, we will make a bargain with you for this right. When the gold or other valuable minerals are taken away, the country will again be yours to dispose of in any manner you may wish."

Spotted Tail took this proposal as a joke. Was the commissioner asking the Indians to *lend* the Black Hills to the white men for a while? His response was to ask Senator Allison if he would lend him a team of mules on such terms.

"It will be hard for our government to keep the whites out of the hills," Allison continued. "To try to do so will give you and our government great trouble, because the whites that may wish to go there are very numerous." The senator's ignorance of the Plains Indians' feeling for the Powder River country was displayed in his next proposal: "There is another country lying far toward the setting sun, over which you roam and hunt, and which territory is [wilderness], extending to the summit of the Bighorn Mountains. . . . It does not seem to be of very great value or use to you, and our people think they would like to have the portion of it I have described."

While Senator Allison's incredible demands were being translated, Red Dog rode up on a pony and announced that he had a message from Red Cloud. The absent Oglala chief requested a week's recess to give the tribes time to hold councils of their own in which to consider all proposals concerning their lands. The commissioners agreed to give the Indians three days.

The idea of giving up their last great hunting ground was so preposterous that none of the chiefs even discussed it during their councils. They did debate very earnestly the question of the Black Hills. Some reasoned that if the United States government had no intention of enforcing the treaty and keeping the white miners out, then perhaps the Indians should demand payment—a great deal of money—for the yellow metal taken from the hills. Others were determined not to sell at any price. The Black Hills belonged to the Indians, they argued. If the Bluecoat soldiers would not drive out the miners, then the warriors must.

On September 23, the commissioners, riding in army ambulances from Camp Robinson and escorted by a larger cavalry troop, again arrived at the council shelter. Red Cloud was there early, and he protested vigorously about the large number of soldiers. Just as he was preparing to give his preliminary speech to the commissioners, a sudden commotion broke out among the warriors far in the distance. About 300 Oglalas who had come in from the Powder River country trotted their ponies down a slope, occasionally firing off rifles. Some were chanting a song in Sioux.

The Black Hills is my land and I love it
And whoever interferes
Will hear this gun.

An Indian mounted on a gray horse forced his way through the ranks of warriors gathered around the canvas shelter. He was Crazy Horse's envoy, Little Big Man, stripped for battle and wearing two revolvers belted to his waist. "I will kill the first chief who speaks for selling the Black Hills!" he shouted. He danced his horse across the open space between the commissioners and the chiefs.

Young-Man-Afraid-of-His-Horses and a group of unofficial
Sioux policemen immediately swarmed around Little Big Man
and moved him away. The chiefs and the commissioners, however, must have guessed that Little Big Man voiced the feelings
of most of the warriors present. General Terry suggested to his
fellow commissioners that they board the army
ambulances and return to the safety of Camp
Robinson.

After giving the Indians a few days to
calm down, the commissioners quietly
arranged a meeting with 20 chiefs in the
headquarters building of the Red Cloud
agency. During three days of speech
making, the chiefs made it quite
clear to the Great Father's representatives that the Black
Hills could not be bought
cheaply, if at any price.
Spotted Tail finally grew

*In 1891, John Nicholas
Choate photographed
Young-Man-Afraid-of-His-
Horses during a visit to the
Carlisle Indian Industrial
School. Choate became
famous as the photogra-
pher of life at this boarding
school for Sioux children in
Carlisle, Pennsylvania. [LOC,
USZ62-107821]*

impatient with the commissioners and asked them to submit a definite proposal in writing.

The offer was $400,000 a year for the mineral rights; or if the Sioux wished to sell the hills outright, the price would be $6 million, payable in 15 annual installments. (This was a markdown price indeed. One Black Hills mine alone would later yield more than $500 million in gold.)

Red Cloud did not even appear for the final meeting. He let Spotted Tail speak for all the Sioux. Spotted Tail firmly rejected both offers. The Black Hills were not for lease or for sale.

The commissioners packed up, returned to Washington, reported their failure, and recommended that Congress disregard the wishes of the Indians and make a payment "as a fair equivalent of the value of the hills." This forced purchase of the Black Hills should be "presented to the Indians as a finality," they said.

Thus was set in motion a chain of actions that would bring the greatest defeat ever suffered by the United States Army in its wars with the Indians and ultimately would destroy forever the freedom of the northern Plains Indians.

It began with a recommendation written on November 9, 1875, by E. C. Watkins, special inspector for the Office of Indian Affairs. He wrote that nonagency Indians were a threat to the reservation system and that troops should be sent to "*whip* them into subjection." This led Commissioner of Indian Affairs Edward P. Smith to order all nonreservation Indians to report to agencies by January 31, 1876. If they did not, a "military force would be sent to compel them."

When runners went out from the agencies late in December to warn the non-agency chiefs to come in, heavy snows blanketed the northern Plains. Blizzards and severe cold made it impossible for some couriers to return until weeks after the January 31 deadline. It would have been impossible to move women and children by ponies and travois. And, had the "hostiles" somehow managed to reach the agencies, they would have starved there. Reservation food supplies were so low that hundreds of Indians left in March to go north in search of game to supplement their meager government rations.

Philip Sheridan in a photograph probably taken in 1865 when he was a major general. In 1869 he was promoted to lieutenant general and made commander of the Military Division of the Missouri, which was responsible for the northern plains. In January of that year, Sheridan was introduced to the Comanche chief Tosawi, who was surrendering his band. Tosawi pointed to himself and said in broken English, "Tosawi good Indian." Sheridan replied, "The only good Indians I ever saw were dead." His quote was later turned into "The only good Indian is a dead Indian."
[LOC, DIG-cwpbh-01010]

It was in the Moon of the Dark Red Calves (February) that the government decided to act. On February 7, after the deadline had expired, Secretary of War William W. Belknap authorized Lieutenant General Philip Sheridan, commander of the military district that included the Sioux lands, to begin military operations against the "hostile Sioux." The next day, General Sheridan issued his orders. The Bluecoats' campaign against Sitting Bull, Crazy Horse, and their allies had begun.

The January 31 ultimatum had been basically a declaration of war against the independent Indians, and many of them had accepted it as that. But they had not expected the Bluecoats to strike as soon as they did. In the Moon of the Snowblind (March), Brigadier General George Crook, called Three

Brigadier General George Crook in an undated photograph. [LOC, DIG-cwpbh-03770]

Stars Crook, came marching north with his men from Fort Fetterman along the old Bozeman Trail.

About this time, a band of Northern Cheyenne and Oglala Sioux left Red Cloud's agency to go to the Powder River country, where they hoped to find a few buffalo and antelope. About the middle of March, they joined some nonagency Indians, both Sioux and Cheyenne, camped a few miles from where the Little Powder River runs into the Powder River. Two Moon was among the Cheyenne leaders.

Without warning, at dawn on March 17, a cavalry force under the command of Colonel Joseph J. Reynolds attacked this peaceful camp. Fearing nothing in their own country, the Indians were asleep when two troops of cavalry dashed into the tepee village, firing pistols and rifles. At the same time, a third troop swept away the Indians' horse herd.

The first reaction from the warriors was to get as many villagers as possible out of the way of the soldiers, who were firing recklessly in all directions. As the women, children, and elderly scrambled and hobbled up a rugged mountain slope, the warriors took positions on ledges or behind huge rocks. From these places they kept the soldiers at bay until the others could escape across the Powder River.

The Bluecoats burned the tepees with everything in them, destroyed all the pemmican and saddles in the camp, and drove away almost every pony the Indians owned. As soon as darkness fell, the warriors went to where the Bluecoats were camped, determined to recover their stolen horses. Two Moon described what happened next: "That night the soldiers slept, leaving the horses to one side; so we crept up and stole them back again, and then we went away."

Three Stars Crook was so angry at Colonel Reynolds for allowing the Indians to escape from their village and recover their horses that he ordered him court-martialed. The army reported this foray as "the attack on Crazy Horse's village," but Crazy Horse was miles away to the northeast. It took Two Moon and the other survivors more than three days to reach his camp.

A photograph of Joseph J. Reynolds taken during the Civil War. [LOC, DIG-ppmsca-22323]

Crazy Horse received the cold, starving fugitives hospitably, gave them robes and food, and found room for them in the Oglala tepees. "I'm glad you are come," he said to Two Moon after listening to accounts of the Bluecoats plundering the village. "We are going to fight the white man again."

"All right," Two Moon replied. "I am ready to fight. I have fought already. My people have been killed, my horses stolen; I am satisfied to fight."

In the Geese Laying Moon (April), when the grass was tall and the horses were strong,

Crazy Horse broke camp and led the Oglalas and Cheyenne north to the mouth of the Tongue River, where Sitting Bull and the Hunkpapas had been living through the winter. Not long after that, a chief named Lame Deer arrived with a band of Minneconjous and asked permission to camp nearby. They had heard about all the Bluecoats marching through the Sioux hunting grounds and wanted to be near Sitting Bull's powerful band of Hunkpapas should there be any trouble.

As the weather warmed, the tribes began moving northward in search of wild game and fresh grass. Along the way, they were joined by bands of Brulés, Sans Arcs, Blackfoot Sioux, and additional Cheyenne. Most of these Indians had left their reservations in accordance with their treaty rights as hunters. Those who had heard of the January 31 ultimatum either considered it only another idle threat of the Great Father's agents or did not believe it applied to peaceful Indians.

NINE

Victory at Little Bighorn

The chargers are coming! They are charging!
The chargers are coming!

—Sioux criers announcing the attack by Major Marcus Reno

WHILE THESE SEVERAL THOUSAND INDIANS were camped on the Rosebud River, many young warriors joined them from the reservations. They brought rumors of great forces of Bluecoats marching from three directions. Three Stars Crook was coming from the south. The One Who Limps (Colonel John Gibbon, commander of troops in a fort in southeast Montana Territory) was coming from the west. One Star Terry and Long Hair Custer were coming from the east.

Early in the Moon of Making Fat (June), the Hunkpapas had their annual Sun Dance. For three days, Sitting Bull danced, bled himself, and stared at the sun until he fell into a trance and had a vision. When

A photograph of John Gibbon taken in 1864, when he was a brigadier general. Gibbon was reduced to his permanent rank of colonel after the Civil War. He got his Indian name the One Who Limps because of wounds he suffered in the Civil War. [LOC, DIG-cwpb-04455]

he rose again, he spoke to his people. In his vision he had heard the voice of Wakantanka the Great Spirit crying, "I give you these because they have no ears." When he looked into the sky he saw soldiers falling like grasshoppers, with their heads down and their hats falling off. They were falling right into the Indian camp. Because the white men had no ears and would not listen, Wakantanka the Great Spirit was giving these soldiers to the Indians to be killed.

A few days later, a hunting party of Cheyenne sighted a column of Bluecoats camped for the night in the valley of the

An 1876 Frank Leslie's Illustrated Newspaper *woodcut showing a portion of General Crook's army crossing a river the day before it would fight in the Battle of the Rosebud. [LOC, USZ62-74804]*

Rosebud River. The hunters rode back to camp, sounding the wolf howl of danger. Three Stars was coming.

The different chiefs sent criers through their villages and then held hasty councils. It was decided to leave about half the warriors to protect the villages while the others would travel through the night and attack Three Stars and his soldiers the next morning. About a thousand Sioux and Cheyenne formed the war party. A few women went along to help with the spare horses. Sitting Bull, Crazy Horse, and Two Moon were among the leaders.

For a long time, Crazy Horse had been waiting for a chance to test himself in battle with the Bluecoats. In the years since the Fetterman fight at Fort Phil Kearny, he had studied the soldiers and their ways of fighting. Each time he went into the Black Hills to seek visions, he had asked Wakantanka to give him secret powers so that he would know how to lead the Oglalas to victory if the white men ever came again to make war upon his people. Since the time of his youth, Crazy Horse had believed that the world men lived in was only a shadow of the real world. To get into the real world, he had to dream. When he was in the real world, everything seemed to float or dance. His horse danced as if it were wild or crazy, and this was why he called himself Crazy Horse. He had learned that if he dreamed himself into the real world before going into a fight, he could endure anything.

On this day, June 17, 1876, after Crazy Horse dreamed himself into the real world, he showed the Sioux how to do many things they had never done before while fighting the white

An 1876 Frank Leslie's Illustrated Newspaper *woodcut drawing of a scene from the Battle of the Rosebud. [LOC, USZ62-54652]*

man's soldiers. When Crook sent his cavalry, the Sioux didn't rush forward into the blaze of bullets—instead, they rode toward both ends of the Bluecoats' lines and struck where the soldiers were weakest. Crazy Horse kept his warriors mounted and always moving. By the time the sun was in the top of the sky (noon), he had the soldiers mixed up in three separate fights. By making many darting charges on their swift ponies, the Sioux kept the soldiers apart and always on the defensive. When the Bluecoats' gunfire grew too overwhelming, the Sioux would draw away, tantalize a few soldiers into pursuit, and then turn on them with a fury.

The Cheyenne also distinguished themselves that day, especially in the dangerous charges. A chief named Comes-in-Sight was the bravest of all, but as he was swinging his horse about after a charge into the soldiers' flank, the animal was shot down in front of a Bluecoat infantry line. Suddenly another Cheyenne horse and rider galloped out and swerved to shield Chief Comes-in-Sight from the soldiers' fire. In a moment Comes-in-Sight was up behind the rider. The rescuer was his sister Buffalo-Calf-Road-Woman, who had come along to help with the horse herds. That was why the Cheyennes always remembered this fight as the Battle Where the Girl Saved Her Brother. The white men called it the Battle of the Rosebud.

When the sun went down, the fighting ended. The Indians knew they had given Three Stars a good fight, but they did not know until the next morning that they had whipped him. At first daylight, Sioux and Cheyenne scouts went out along the ridges, and they could see the Bluecoat column retreating to the south. General Crook was returning to his base camp on Goose Creek to await reinforcements or a message from Gibbon, Terry, or Custer. The Indians on the Rosebud were too strong for one column of soldiers.

The chiefs now decided to move west to the valley of the Greasy Grass (Little Bighorn River). Scouts had come in with reports of great herds of antelope west of there, and they said grass for the horses was plentiful. Soon the camp circles were spread along the west bank of the twisting Greasy Grass for almost three miles. No one knew how many Indians were there, but the number could not have been less than 10,000 people, including 3,000 or 4,000 warriors.

The time was early in the Moon When the Chokecherries Are Ripe (August). Hunting parties were coming and going in the direction of the nearby Bighorn Mountains, where they had found a few buffalo as well as antelope. The women were digging wild turnips out on the prairies. Every night one or more of the tribal circles held dances, and some nights the chiefs met in councils.

Sitting Bull did not believe the victory on the Rosebud had fulfilled his prophecy of soldiers falling into the Indian camp. Since the retreat of Three Stars, however, no hunting parties had sighted any Bluecoats between the Powder and the Bighorn rivers.

But Long Hair Custer was prowling along the Rosebud. On the morning of June 25, scouts reported that his soldiers had crossed the last high ridge between the Rosebud and the Indian camp and were marching toward the Little Bighorn River.

When they got near the Indian camp, Long Hair divided his force into three groups. Long Hair commanded one group. Subordinates Major Marcus Reno and Major Frederick Benteen commanded the other two.

Pte-San-Waste-Win (Pretty Gray Cow), a cousin of Sitting Bull, was one of the young women digging turnips that morning. She remembered the soldiers were six to eight miles distant when first sighted. "We could see the flashing of their sabers and saw that there were very many soldiers in the party." The soldiers seen by Pte-San-Waste-Win and other Indians in the middle of the camp were those in Custer's force. These Indians were not aware of Major Marcus Reno's attack against the south end of camp until they heard rifle fire from the direction of the Blackfoot Sioux lodges.

Black Elk, then a 13-year-old Oglala boy, was swimming with his companions in the Little Bighorn. The sun was straight above, and it was getting very hot when he heard a crier shouting in the Hunkpapa camp, "The chargers are coming! They are charging! The chargers are coming!" The warning was repeated by an Oglala crier, and Black Elk could hear the cry going from camp to camp northward to the Cheyennes.

Chief Iron Thunder, a brother of Hump, was in the Minneconjou camp. "I did not know anything about Reno's attack until his men were so close that the bullets went through the camp, and everything was in confusion. The horses were so frightened we could not catch them."

Crow King, one of Sitting Bull's war chiefs who was in the Hunkpapa camp, said that Reno's cavalry commenced firing at about 400 yards' distance. The Hunkpapas and Blackfoot Sioux retreated slowly on foot to give the women and children time to go to a place of safety. At the same time, other warriors were gathering what horses they could for a cavalry charge counterattack. "By that time, we had warriors enough to turn upon the whites," Crow King said.

Two Moon ordered the Cheyenne warriors to get their horses and then told the women to take cover away from the tepee village. "I rode swiftly toward Sitting Bull's camp. Then I saw the white soldiers fighting in a line," he said. The battle quickly became chaotic, with Sioux warriors and soldiers mixed together, and everyone shooting at one another. Two Moon said, "The air was full of smoke and dust. I saw the soldiers fall back and drop into the riverbed like buffalo fleeing."

The war chief who rallied the Indians and turned back Reno's attack was a muscular, full-chested, 36-year-old Hunkpapa—none other than Gall. Gall had grown up in the tribe as an orphan. While still a young man he had distinguished himself as a hunter and warrior, and Sitting Bull had adopted him as a younger brother. Some years before, while the commissioners were attempting to persuade the Sioux to take up farming as a part of the treaty of 1868, Gall went to Fort Rice to speak for the Hunkpapas. "We were born naked," he said, "and have been taught to hunt and live on the game. You tell us that we must learn to farm, live in one house, and take on your ways. Suppose the people living beyond the great sea should come and tell you that you must stop farming and kill your cattle, and take your houses and lands, what would you

Battle of the Little Bighorn

Crazy Horse attack

Little Bighorn River

Custer killed

Custer advance

MONTANA TERRITORY

Cheyenne camp

Gall attacks

Sioux camp

Reno and Benteen forces under siege

Reno retreat

Reno advance

△ Indian camps
☆ Battles
Indian attacks
Cavalry advances
Cavalry retreat
River

Miles
0   1/4   1/2

N W E S

do? Would you not fight them?" In the decade following that speech, nothing changed Gall's opinion of the white man's self-righteous arrogance, and by the summer of 1876, he was generally accepted by the Hunkpapas as Sitting Bull's lieutenant, the war chief of the tribe.

Reno's first onrush caught several women and children in the open, and the cavalry's flying bullets wiped out Gall's family. "It made my heart bad," he told a newspaperman some years later. "After that I killed all my enemies with the hatchet."

Custer split his force into three parts to attack the Indian camp from different sides. But his attack was not coordinated, and the three individual forces were too small to defend themselves. Reno and his men survived only because they were able to retreat and rejoin Benteen's force. Custer and his men, surrounded by Crazy Horse's and Gall's warriors, were wiped out.

Charles M. Russell's 1903 painting of the Battle of Little Bighorn. [LOC, USZC4-7160]

His description of the tactics used to block Reno was equally blunt: "Sitting Bull and I were at the point where Reno attacked. Sitting Bull was big medicine. The women and children were hastily moved downstream. . . . The women and children caught the horses for the bucks to mount them; the bucks mounted and charged back Reno and checked him, and drove him into the timber."

In other words, Gall and his warriors overwhelmed one end of Reno's defensive line. Reno tried to get his soldiers to retreat into some nearby woods. But Gall's warriors quickly turned the organized retreat into a panic-stricken rush to safety. This made it possible for Gall to divert hundreds of warriors for a frontal attack against Custer's column, while Crazy Horse and Two Moon struck the sides and rear.

Kill Eagle, a Blackfoot Sioux chief, later said that the movement of Indians toward Custer's column was "like a hurricane . . . like bees swarming out of a hive." Young Black Elk, watching from across the river, could see a big dust cloud whirling on the hill, and then horses began coming out of it with empty saddles.

Crow King said that all the soldiers dismounted when the Indians surrounded them. "We crowded them toward our main camp and killed them all. They kept in order and fought like brave warriors as long as they had a man left."

According to Lakota chief Red Horse, toward the end of the fighting with Custer, "these soldiers became foolish, many throwing away their guns and raising their hands, saying, 'Sioux, pity us; take us prisoners.' The Sioux did not take a single soldier prisoner, but killed all of them; none were alive for even a few minutes."

Long after the battle, White Bull of the Minneconjou drew four pictographs showing himself grappling with and killing a soldier identified as Custer. Among others who claimed to have killed Custer were Rain-in-the-Face, Flat Hip, and Brave Bear. Red Horse said that an unidentified Santee warrior killed Custer. Most Indians who told of the battle said they never saw Custer and did not know who killed him.

In an interview later given in Canada, Sitting Bull said that he never saw Custer, but that other Indians had seen and recognized him just before he was killed. Sitting Bull did not say who killed Custer.

Custer's death in the Battle of Little Bighorn inspired many illustrations of the event. Almost all were inaccurate, and the worst of them, like this 1878 lithograph titled General Custer's Death Struggle, *were highly romanticized interpretations of what happened.* [LOC, DIG-pga-04166]

An Arapaho warrior who was riding with the Cheyenne said that Custer was killed by several Indians. "He was dressed in buckskin, coat and pants, and was on his hands and knees. He had been shot through the side, and there was blood coming from his mouth. He seemed to be watching the Indians moving around him. Four soldiers were sitting up around him, but they were all badly wounded. All the other soldiers were down. Then the Indians closed in around him, and I did not see any more."

Regardless of who had killed him, Long Hair, who made the Thieves' Road into the Black Hills, was dead with all his men. Reno's soldiers, however, reinforced by those of Major Frederick Benteen, were dug in on a hill farther down the river. The Indians surrounded the hill and watched the soldiers through the night, and the next morning started fighting them again. During the day, scouts sent out by the chiefs came back with warnings of many more soldiers marching in the direction of the Little Bighorn.

After a council it was decided to break camp. The warriors had shot most of their ammunition, and they knew it would be foolish to try to fight so many soldiers with bows and arrows. Before sunset they started up the valley toward the Bighorn Mountains, the tribes separating along the way and taking different directions. Thus ended the Battle of Little Bighorn.

When the white men in the East heard of Long Hair's defeat, they called it a massacre and went crazy with anger. Because they could not punish Sitting Bull and the war chiefs, the Great Council in Washington (Congress) decided to punish the Indians they could find—those who remained on the reservations and had taken no part in the fighting.

An 1893 photograph of Sioux chief Rain-in-the-Face, one of the warriors who fought in the Battle of Little Bighorn. His participation in the battle inspired Henry Wadsworth Longfellow to write the poem "The Revenge of Rain-in-the-Face," published in 1878. [LOC, USZ62-104681]

On July 22, 1876, Great Warrior Sherman received authority to assume military control of all reservations in the Sioux country and to treat the Indians there as prisoners of war. On August 15 the Great Council made a new law requiring the Indians to give up all rights to the Powder River country and the Black Hills. They did this without regard to the Sioux Treaty of 1868, claiming that the Indians had violated the treaty by going to war with the United States. This was difficult for the reservation Indians to understand because they had not attacked United States soldiers, nor had Sitting Bull's followers attacked them until Custer sent Reno charging through the Sioux villages.

To keep the reservation Indians peaceful, a new commission was sent in

September to flatter and threaten the chiefs and secure their signatures to legal documents transferring the great wealth of the Black Hills to white ownership. Several members of this commission were old hands at stealing Indian lands. They included Newton Edmunds, the Reverend Samuel D. Hinman, and Bishop Henry Whipple, who had also worked as a missionary among the Sioux. At the Red Cloud agency, Bishop Whipple opened the proceedings with a prayer, and then the chairman, who was named George Manypenny, read the new conditions laid down by Congress. Because these conditions were stated in the usual confusing language of lawmakers, Bishop Whipple attempted to explain them in phrases that could be used by the interpreters.

> *My heart has for many years been very warm toward the red man. We came here to bring a message to you from your Great Father, and there are certain things we have given to you in his exact words. We cannot alter them even to the scratch of a pen. . . . When the Great Council made the appropriation [spent money] this year to continue your supplies they made certain provisions, three in number, and unless they were complied with no more appropriations would be made by Congress. Those three provisions are: First, that you shall give up the Black Hills country and the country to the north; second, that you shall receive your rations on the Missouri River; and third, that the Great Father shall be permitted to locate three roads from the Missouri River across the reservation to that new country*

where the Black Hills are. . . . The Great Father said that his heart was full of tenderness for his red children, and he selected this commission of friends of the Indians that they might devise a plan, as he directed them, in order that the Indian nations might be saved, and that instead of growing smaller and smaller until the last Indian looks upon his own grave, they might become as the white man has become, a great and powerful people.

To Bishop Whipple's listeners, this seemed a strange way indeed to save the Indian nations, taking their Black Hills and hunting grounds and moving their people far away to the Missouri River. Most of the chiefs knew that it was already too late to save the Black Hills. But they protested strongly against having their reservations moved to the Missouri River.

One chief remembered that the Great Father had promised that they would never be moved, yet they had been moved five times. "I think you had better put the Indians on wheels," he said bitterly, "and you can run them about whenever you wish."

Spotted Tail accused the government and the commissioners of betraying the Indians; he spoke of broken promises and false words. "This war did not spring up here in our land; this war was brought upon us by the children of the Great Father, who came to take our land from us without price, and who, in our land, do a great many evil things. . . . This war has come from robbery—from the stealing of our land."

The commissioners gave the Indians a week to discuss the terms among themselves. It soon became evident that the Sioux were not going to sign anything. The chiefs pointed out that the Sioux Treaty of 1868 required the signatures of three-fourths of the male adults of the Sioux tribes to change anything in it, and more than half of the warriors were in the north with Sitting Bull and Crazy Horse. In reply to this, the commissioners explained that only friendly reservation Indians were covered by the treaty. Most of the chiefs did not accept this. To break down their opposition, the commissioners dropped strong hints that unless they signed, the Great Council in its anger would cut off all rations immediately, they would be removed to the Indian Territory (Oklahoma) in the south, and the army would take all their guns and horses.

There was no way out. The Black Hills were stolen. The Powder River country and its herds of wild game were gone. Without either wild game or rations, the people would starve. The thought of moving far away to a strange country in the south was unbearable, and if the army took their guns and ponies, they would no longer be men.

Red Cloud and his subchiefs signed first, and then Spotted Tail and his people. After that the commissioners went to the other agencies and reservations and badgered the Sioux tribes there into signing. Thus did Paha Sapa, its spirits and its mysteries, its vast pine forests, and its billion dollars in gold, pass forever from the hands of the Indians into the domain of the United States.

TEN

The Death of
Crazy Horse

One does not sell the earth upon which the people walk.
—CRAZY HORSE OF THE OGLALA SIOUX

MEANWHILE, UNITED STATES ARMY TROOPS under
Three Stars Crook, thirsting for revenge,
were prowling the country north and west
of the Black Hills, killing Indians
wherever they could be found. On
September 9, 1876, near Slim
Buttes, a force under the command of a captain named
Anson Mills stumbled upon
a village of Oglalas and Minneconjous. Captain Mills attacked, but all the Indians
escaped except the village
chief, American Horse, four
warriors, and fifteen women
and children, who were trapped

Chief American Horse. [LOC, USZ62-102186]

131

in a cave at the end of a small canyon. American Horse and two others were killed; the rest were taken prisoner.

Three Stars Crook and his main body arrived and began destroying the village. Meanwhile some of the Sioux who had escaped reached Sitting Bull's camp and told him what had happened. Sitting Bull and Gall, with about 600 warriors, immediately went to help, but they arrived too late. Although Sitting Bull counterattacked, his warriors had so little ammunition that the Bluecoats held them off with rearguard actions while the main column marched on to the Black Hills.

When the soldiers were gone, Sitting Bull and his warriors went into American Horse's devastated village, rescued the few survivors, and buried the dead.

In an effort to get as far away from the soldiers as possible, Sitting Bull took his people north along the Yellowstone River, where buffalo could be found. In the Moon of Falling Leaves (October), Gall went out with a hunting party and came upon an army wagon train. The soldiers were taking supplies to Fort Keogh, a new fort they were building where the Tongue River flowed into the Yellowstone River.

Gall's warriors ambushed the wagon train near Glendive Creek and captured 60 mules. As soon as Sitting Bull heard about the wagon train and the new fort, he sent for Johnny Brughiere, a half-breed who had joined his camp. Brughiere knew how to write, and Sitting Bull told him to put down on a piece of paper some words he had to say to the commander of the soldiers.

I want to know what you are doing on this road. You scare all the buffalo away. I want to hunt in this place. I want you to turn back from here. If you don't, I will fight you again. I want you to leave what you have got here, and turn back from here. I am your friend.

—Sitting Bull

Nelson A. Miles in a photograph taken in late 1864 or 1865 when he was a major general. Miles was a Civil War hero and received the Medal of Honor for his action in the Battle of Chancellorsville. His wife was a niece of General William Tecumseh Sherman. [LOC, DIG-cwpbh-00846]

When Lieutenant Colonel Elwell Otis, who was commanding the wagon train, received the message, he sent a scout with a reply. The soldiers were going to Fort Keogh, Otis said, and many more soldiers were coming to join them. If Sitting Bull wanted a fight, the soldiers would give him one.

Sitting Bull did not want a fight. He wanted only to be left alone to hunt buffalo. He sent a warrior out with a white flag, asking for a talk with the soldier chief. By this time, a colonel named Nelson A. Miles and more soldiers had joined the train. As Colonel Miles had been searching for Sitting Bull since the end of summer, he immediately agreed to a parley.

They met on October 20 between a line of soldiers and a line of warriors. Miles was escorted by an officer and five men, Sitting Bull by a subchief and five warriors. The day was very cold, and Miles was wearing a long coat trimmed with bear fur. Because of this, he was now Bear Coat to the Indians.

With Johnny Brughiere interpreting, Bear Coat began the meeting by accusing Sitting Bull of always being against the white man and his ways. Sitting Bull admitted that he was not for the whites, but neither was he an enemy to them as long as they left him alone. Bear Coat wanted to know what Sitting Bull was doing in the Yellowstone country. The question was a foolish one, but the Hunkpapa answered it politely: he was hunting buffalo to feed and clothe his people. Bear Coat then made passing mention of a reservation for the Hunkpapas, but Sitting Bull brushed it aside. He would spend the winter in the Black Hills, he said. The parley ended with nothing resolved. The two men agreed to meet again the next day.

The second meeting quickly became a succession of disagreements. Sitting Bull began by saying that he had not fought the soldiers until they came to fight him. He promised that there would be no more fighting if the white men would take their soldiers and forts out of the Indians' country. Bear Coat replied that there could be no peace for the Sioux until they were all on reservations. At this, Sitting Bull became angry. He declared that the Great Spirit had made him an Indian but not an agency Indian, and he did not intend to become one. He ended the conference abruptly and returned to his warriors, ordering them to scatter because he suspected that Bear Coat's soldiers would try to attack. The soldiers did open fire. This fight, known as the Battle of Cedar Creek, was short—the Hunkpapas fought only long enough to let their women, children, and old people escape.

By springtime of 1877, Sitting Bull was tired of running. He decided there was no longer room enough for white men and the Sioux to live together in the Great Father's country. He would take his people to Canada, to the land of the British Grandmother, Queen Victoria.

Meanwhile, General Crook and his army were looking for Crazy Horse. Instead his troops found the Cheyenne village of Dull Knife. Most of these Cheyenne had not been in the Little Bighorn battle but had slipped away from Red Cloud's reservation in search of food after the army took possession there and stopped their rations. Against this village of 150 lodges, General Crook sent Colonel Ranald S. Mackenzie, a successful Indian fighter in the southern Plains and known to the Indians as Bad Hand or Three Fingers because of wounds suffered while fighting in the Civil War.

It was the Deer Rutting Moon (November) and very cold, with deep snow in the shaded places and ice-crusted snow in the open places. Mackenzie and his troops struck the Cheyenne at first daylight. The Pawnee mercenaries went in first. They caught the Cheyenne in the lodges, killing many of them as they awakened. Others ran out naked into the biting cold, the warriors trying to fight off the Pawnees and the onrushing soldiers long enough for their women and children to escape.

Dull Knife and Little Wolf managed to form a rear guard. Soon, their ammunition exhausted, they broke away to join their women and children fleeing toward the Bighorns. Behind them Mackenzie and his troops burned the lodges and shot the captured horses.

Meanwhile, the survivors struggled to reach Crazy Horse's camp. During the first night of flight, 12 infants and several old people froze to death. The next night, the men killed some of the ponies, disemboweled them, and thrust small children inside to keep them from freezing. The old people put their hands and feet in beside the children. For three days they tramped across the snow, their bare feet leaving a trail of blood, and finally reached Crazy Horse's camp.

Crazy Horse shared food, blankets, and shelter with Dull Knife's people, but warned them to be ready to run. The Oglalas did not have enough ammunition left to stand and fight. With Bear Coat Miles searching in the north and Three Stars Crook coming from the south, they would have to leave.

In the Moon of Popping Trees (December), Crazy Horse moved the camp north along the Tongue to a hiding place not far from the new Fort Keogh, where Bear Coat was wintering his soldiers. Cold and hunger became so unbearable for the children and old people that some of the chiefs told Crazy Horse it was time to go and parley with Bear Coat. Their women and children were crying for food, and they needed warm shelters. Crazy Horse knew that Bear Coat wanted to make prisoners of them on a reservation, but he agreed that the chiefs should go. He went with the party, about 30 chiefs and warriors, to a hill not far from the fort. Eight chiefs and warriors volunteered to ride down to the fort, one of them carrying a large white cloth on a lance. As they neared the fort, some mercenary Crows who were working for Bear Coat came charging out. Ignoring the truce flag, the Crows fired point-blank into the Sioux. Only three of the eight escaped alive. Some of the Sioux watching from the hill wanted to ride out and seek revenge, but Crazy Horse insisted that they hurry back to camp. They would have to pack up and run again. Now that Bear Coat knew there were Sioux nearby, he would come searching through the snow for them.

Bear Coat caught up with them on the morning of January 8, 1877, at Battle Butte (known to the white men as the Battle of Wolf Mountain). He sent his soldiers charging through foot-deep snow. Crazy Horse had only a little ammunition left, but

Frank Leslie's Illustrated Newspaper *published this woodcut illustration of the Battle of Wolf Mountain a few months after the event in 1877. [LOC, USZ62-109592]*

he had good warriors, including Little Big Man, who knew enough tricks to mislead and punish the soldiers while the main body of Indians escaped through the Wolf Mountains toward the Bighorns. For four hours they kept the soldiers stumbling and falling over ice-covered cliffs. Snow began sifting down during the engagement, and by early afternoon a blizzard was raging. This was enough for Bear Coat. He took his men back to the warmth of Fort Keogh.

Through the screen of sleety snow, Crazy Horse and his people made their way to the familiar country of the Little Powder River. They were camped there in February, living off what game they could find, when runners brought news that Spotted Tail and a party of Brulés were coming from the south.

During the cold moons, Three Stars Crook had taken his men out of the snow into Fort Fetterman. While he was waiting for spring, he paid a visit to Spotted Tail and promised him that the reservation Sioux would not have to move to the Missouri River if the Brulé chief could find Crazy Horse and persuade him to surrender.

Just before Spotted Tail arrived, Crazy Horse told his father that he was going away. He asked his father to shake hands with Spotted Tail and tell him the Oglalas would come in as soon as the weather made it possible for women and children to travel. Then he went off to the Bighorns alone to think.

When Spotted Tail arrived, he guessed that Crazy Horse was avoiding him. He sent messengers out to find the Oglala leader, but Crazy Horse had vanished in the deep snows. Before Spotted Tail returned to Nebraska, however, he convinced Crazy

Horse's ally, Chief Big Foot, that he should surrender his Minneconjous, and he received promises from Crazy Horse's cousin Chief Touch-the-Clouds and three other chiefs that they would bring their people to the reservation early in the spring.

On April 14, Touch-the-Clouds, with a large number of Minneconjous and Sans Arcs from Crazy Horse's village, arrived at the Spotted Tail agency and surrendered. A few days before this happened, Three Stars Crook had sent Red Cloud out to find Crazy Horse and promise him that if he surrendered, a reservation would be created for him in the Powder River country. On April 27, Red Cloud met Crazy Horse and told him of Three Stars's promise. Crazy Horse's 900 Oglalas were starving, the warriors had no ammunition, and their horses were thin and bony. Crazy Horse decided to lead his people to Camp Robinson and surrender.

The last of the Sioux war chiefs now became a reservation Indian, disarmed, dismounted, with no authority over his people, a prisoner of the army, which had never defeated him in battle. Yet he was still a hero to the young men. This adulation made the older agency chiefs jealous.

Late in the summer, Crazy Horse heard that Three Stars Crook wanted him to go to Washington for a council with the Great Father. Crazy Horse refused to go. He could see no point in talking about the promised reservation. He had seen what happened to chiefs like Red Cloud and Spotted Tail who went to the Great Father's house in Washington; they came back fat from the white man's way of living and with all the hardness gone out of them. Crazy Horse did not want that to

This 1877 woodcut engraving from Frank Leslie's Illustrated Newspaper *shows Crazy Horse's band traveling to surrender to General Crook at the Red Cloud agency. In the lower right-hand corner, note the travois built to carry small children.* [LOC, USZCN-37]

happen to him. Because of Crazy Horse's continued resistance to the white men, even while he was living on the reservation, the other chiefs resented him.

In August, news came that another Native people, the Nez Percé, were at war with the Bluecoats. At the agencies, soldier chiefs began enlisting warriors to do their scouting for them against the Nez Percé. Crazy Horse told the young men not to go against those other Indians far away, but some would not listen. On August 31, the day these former Sioux warriors put on their Bluecoat uniforms to march away, Crazy Horse was so sick with disgust that he rejected the plan of living on a government reservation created for him. Instead he and his people would return to the Powder River country and live there as free Sioux.

When Three Stars Crook heard of this from his spies, he ordered eight cavalry companies to go after Crazy Horse and arrest him. But before the soldiers arrived, Crazy Horse's friends warned him. Not knowing what the soldiers' purpose was, Crazy Horse told his people to scatter. Then he set out alone to the Spotted Tail agency to seek refuge with his old friend Touch-the-Clouds.

The soldiers found him there, placed him under arrest, and informed him they were taking him back to Camp Robinson to see Three Stars Crook. Upon arrival at the fort, Crazy Horse was told that it was too late to talk with Three Stars that day. He was turned over to a captain named James Kennington and one of the agency policemen. Crazy Horse stared hard at the agency policeman. It was Little Big Man, who not so long ago had defied the commissioners who came to steal Paha Sapa, the same Little Big Man who had threatened to kill the first chief who spoke for selling the Black Hills, the brave Little Big Man who had last fought beside Crazy Horse on the icy slopes of the Wolf Mountains against Bear Coat Miles. Now the white men had bought Little Big Man and made him into an agency policeman.

Guided by his escort, Crazy Horse walked toward a building. Its windows were barred with iron, and Crazy Horse could see men behind the bars with chains on their legs. It was a trap for an animal, and Crazy Horse lunged away with Little Big

In the mid-1970s Crazy Horse was commemorated on a first-class postage stamp. Unlike other chiefs, Crazy Horse refused to let himself be photographed because he believed the camera would steal or imprison his soul. This portrait, created after his death, is based on a description given by Crazy Horse's sister.

Man holding on to his arm. The scuffling went on for only a few seconds. Someone shouted a command, and then Private William Gentles, a soldier guard following behind them, thrust his bayonet deep into Crazy Horse's abdomen.

Crazy Horse died that night, September 5, 1877, at the age of 35. At dawn the next day, the soldiers presented the dead chief to his father and mother. They put the body of Crazy Horse into a wooden box, fastened it to a pony-drawn travois, and carried it to the Spotted Tail agency, where they mounted it on a scaffold. All through the Drying Grass Moon (September), mourners watched beside the burial place. And then in the Moon of Falling Leaves (October) came the heartbreaking news: the reservation Sioux must leave Nebraska and go to a new reservation on the Missouri River.

Through the crisp, dry autumn of 1877, long lines of exiled Indians driven by soldiers marched northeast toward the barren land. Along the way, several bands slipped away from the column and turned northwest, determined to escape to Canada and join Sitting Bull. With them went the father and mother of Crazy Horse, carrying the heart and bones of their son. At a place known only to them, they buried Crazy Horse somewhere near Chankpe Opi Wakpala, the creek called Wounded Knee.

ELEVEN

Sitting Bull Returns Home

I feel that my country has gotten a bad name, and I want it to have a good name; it used to have a good name; and I sit sometimes and wonder who it is that has given it a bad name.
—SITTING BULL OF THE HUNKPAPA SIOUX

BY 1878, THE SIOUX were living on land between the Missouri River and Black Hills believed to be worthless by the surveyors who had marked off the new east-west boundaries. But even that "worthless" land was about to come under threat.

A great wave of emigration from northern Europe poured into the eastern part of the Dakota Territory, up to the Missouri River boundary of the Great Sioux Reservation. At Bismarck, on the Missouri, a westward-pushing railroad was blocked by the reservation. Settlers bound for Montana and the Northwest clamored for roads to be built across it. Promoters eager for cheap land to be sold to immigrants at high profits hatched schemes to break up the Great Sioux Reservation.

In the old days the Sioux would have fought to keep them out. But now they were disarmed, dismounted, unable even to feed and clothe themselves. Their greatest surviving war leader, Sitting Bull, was an exile in Canada.

Free in Canada, Sitting Bull was a dangerous symbol of subversion to the United States government. The army became frantic in its attempts to force the Hunkpapa leader and his followers to return. In September 1877, the War Department arranged with the Canadian government for General Alfred Terry and a special commission to cross the border under the escort of the Royal Canadian Mounted Police and meet with Sitting Bull at Fort Walsh. One Star Terry planned to promise Sitting Bull a complete pardon, provided he surrendered all firearms and horses and brought his people back to the Hunkpapa agency at Standing Rock.

Sitting Bull was reluctant to meet with Terry. "There is no use in talking to these Americans," he told Commissioner James MacLeod of the mounted police. "They are all liars; you cannot believe anything they say." But Commissioner MacLeod wanted Sitting Bull out of Canada. He finally persuaded the Hunkpapa to come to Fort Walsh on October 17 for a council.

One Star Terry made a short opening speech. "We have come many hundred miles to bring you this message from the Great Father, who, as we have told you before, desires to live in peace with all his people. Too much white and Indian blood has already been shed. It is time that bloodshed should cease."

"What have we done that you should want us to stop?" Sitting Bull retorted. "We have done nothing. It is all the people on your side that have started us to do all these [attacks]. We could not go anywhere else, and so we took refuge in this country." Sitting Bull then talked about the lies and abuse his people had suffered. Then he said, "Go back home where you came from. . . . The part of the country you gave me you ran me out of. I have now come here to stay with these people, and I intend to stay here."

Sitting Bull let several of his followers speak, including a Santee and a Yankton who had joined his band. Their statements reinforced his previous remarks.

After the meeting ended, One Star Terry knew that it was useless to make any further pleas to Sitting Bull. His last hope was Commissioner MacLeod, who agreed to explain the Canadian government's position toward the Hunkpapas. MacLeod informed Sitting Bull that he was an American Indian who had taken refuge in Canada. This meant that Sitting Bull and his people could receive no food or supplies—nothing—from the Canadian government. But nothing MacLeod said changed Sitting Bull's decision. He would remain.

Next morning, One Star Terry started back to the United States.

Sitting Bull and his fellow exiles stayed in Canada four years. Had the Canadian government been more cooperative, they probably would have lived out their lives on the plains of Saskatchewan. But the Canadians viewed Sitting Bull as a potential troublemaker as well as an expensive guest because additional mounted police had to be assigned to watch him. As the seasons passed, a few hungry and ragged families drifted south across the border to surrender at the Sioux agencies in the Dakota Territory.

Sitting Bull begged the Canadians to give his people a reservation where they could support themselves, but he was repeatedly told that he was not a British subject and therefore was not entitled to a land reserve. During the bad winter of 1880, many Sioux horses froze to death. When spring came, more of the exiles began trekking southward on foot. Several of Sitting Bull's most loyal lieutenants, including Gall and Crow King, gave up and headed for the Great Sioux Reservation.

At last, on July 19, 1881, Sitting Bull and 186 of his remaining followers crossed the border and rode into Fort Buford. He looked old and beaten when he surrendered his Winchester rifle to the commanding officer. Instead of sending him to the Hunkpapa agency at Standing Rock, the army broke its promise to give him a pardon and held him at Fort Randall as a military prisoner.

During the late summer of 1881, the return of Sitting Bull was overshadowed by the assassination of Spotted Tail. The murderer was not a white man, but was one of Spotted Tail's own people, Crow Dog. Many Sioux believed it was part of the white man's plot to break the power of the remaining strong chiefs. Agency officials denied this, but suspicions remained.

After the furor over Spotted Tail's death ended, Sioux everywhere on the Great Reservation turned their attention toward Sitting Bull's presence at Fort Randall. Many chiefs and subchiefs came to visit him, wish him well, and do him honor. Newspapermen came to interview him. Instead of being beaten and forgotten as he had thought, Sitting Bull was famous. In 1882 representatives from the different Sioux agencies came to ask his advice concerning a new government proposal to break up the Great Reservation into smaller areas and sell about half

Crow Dog in 1900. [LOC, USZ62-102187]

CROW DOG

the land for white settlement. Sitting Bull advised them not to sell.

Despite their resistance, in 1882 the Sioux came very near to losing 14,000 square miles of territory to a new commission headed by Newton Edmunds, who was an expert at negotiating lands away from Indians. His colleagues were Peter Shannon, a frontier lawyer, and James Teller, a brother of the new secretary of the interior. Accompanying them was a "special interpreter," none other than Reverend Samuel D. Hinman, who had been a missionary to the Sioux since the days of Little Crow.

As the commission traveled from one agency to another, Hinman told the chiefs that he was there to lay out different parts of the reservation for the six agencies. This was necessary, he said, so that the different Sioux tribes could claim the areas as their own and have them as long as they lived. "After we have laid out the reservations," Hinman told Red Cloud, "the Great Father will give you 25,000 cows and 1,000 bulls." To obtain the livestock, however, the Sioux had to sign some papers. As none of the Sioux chiefs could read, they did not know that they were signing away 14,000 square miles of land in exchange for the promised cows and bulls.

At agencies where the Sioux were reluctant to sign anything, Hinman alternately wheedled and bullied them. In order to obtain an abundance of signatures, he persuaded boys as young as seven years old to sign.

Early in 1883, Edmunds and Hinman journeyed to Washington with their bundle of signatures. They succeeded in getting Congress to create a legislative bill that when approved and signed into law would let Edmunds and Hinman take almost half the lands set aside for the Sioux in the 1868 treaty. But the Sioux had, for the moment, some friends in Washington, who questioned the bill. They pointed out that even if all the signatures were legal, Edmunds and Hinman still had not obtained the names of the required three-fourths of all adult male Sioux. Another commission, headed by Senator Henry L. Dawes, was sent to the Dakota Territory to investigate.

During the inquiry, Dawes asked Red Cloud if he believed Reverend Hinman was an honest man. "Mr. Hinman fools you big men," Red Cloud replied.

Red Dog, an Oglala chief who had signed the paper, testified that Hinman had talked about giving them cows and bulls, but had said nothing about the Sioux giving up any land in exchange for them.

Senator Henry Dawes was the sponsor of the General Allotment Act of 1887, commonly called the Dawes Act, which proved to be one of the most disastrous pieces of legislation affecting Native Americans. (See Epilogue) [LOC, DIG-cwpbh-03931]

Little Wound, another Oglala chief who had signed, said, "Mr. Hinman told us that the way the reservation was now no Indian could tell his own ground, and the Great Father and his council thought it best to lay out different reservations and that is the reason we signed the paper."

"Did he say anything about the Great Father having what was left?" asked Senator Dawes.

"No, sir. He did not say anything about that."

Shortly before the Dawes commission came to Dakota, Sitting Bull was released from imprisonment at Fort Randall and transferred to the Hunkpapa agency at Standing Rock. On August 22, 1883, when the commissioners arrived there to hear testimony, he came up to the agency headquarters from his assigned camp on the Grand River to attend the council. The commissioners ignored the presence of the most famous living Sioux chief. Instead they invited testimony from others.

At last, Senator Dawes turned to the interpreter and said, "Ask Sitting Bull if he has anything to say to the committee."

"Of course I will speak to you if you desire me to do so," Sitting Bull responded. "I suppose it is only such men as you desire to speak who must say anything."

"We supposed the Indians would select men to speak for them," Dawes said, "but any man who desires to speak, or any man the Indians here desire shall talk for them, we will be glad to hear if he has anything to say."

"Do you know who I am, that you speak as you do?"

"I know that you are Sitting Bull, and if you have anything to say, we will be glad to hear you."

"Do you recognize me—do you know who I am?"

"I know you are Sitting Bull."

"You say you know I am Sitting Bull, but do you know what position I hold?"

"I do not know any difference between you and the other Indians at this agency."

"I am here by the will of the Great Spirit, and by his will I am a chief. My heart is red and sweet, and I know it is sweet, because whatever passes near me puts out its tongue to me, and yet you men have come here to talk with us, and you say you do not know who I am. I want to tell you that if the Great Spirit has chosen anyone to be the chief of this country, it is myself."

"In whatever capacity you may be here today, if you desire to say anything to us, we will listen to you; otherwise we will dismiss this council."

"Yes, that is all right," Sitting Bull said. "You have conducted yourselves like men who have been drinking whiskey, and I came here to give you some advice." He made a sweeping motion with his hand, and every Indian in the council room arose and followed him out.

Nothing could have dismayed the commissioners more than the thought of the Sioux rallying around a strong leader like Sitting Bull. The government's policy was aimed at eliminating everything Indian among the tribes and making them over into white men. In less than two minutes, they had let Sitting Bull demonstrate his power to block that policy.

Later that day, the other Hunkpapa leaders talked with Sitting Bull. They assured him of their loyalty but told him he should not have offended the commissioners. These men were not like the land thieves who had visited the previous year. These representatives had come to help them keep their land, not to take it away.

Sitting Bull was not so sure about the trustworthiness of any white men, but he said that if he had made a mistake, he was willing to apologize for it. He sent word to the commissioners that he would like another council. He began,

> I am here to apologize to you for my bad conduct, and to take back what I said. I will take it back because I consider I have made your hearts bad. . . . What I take back is what I said to cause the people to leave the council, and want to apologize for leaving myself. . . . Now I will tell you my mind, and I will tell everything straight. I know the Great Spirit is looking down upon me from above and will hear what I say, therefore I will do my best to talk straight; and I am in hopes that someone will listen to my wishes and help me to carry them out.

He then reviewed the history of the Sioux during his lifetime, listing the government's broken promises, but said that he had promised to travel the white man's path and would keep his promises.

Sitting Bull went on to describe the condition of the Indians. They had none of the things that white men had. If they were to become like white men, they must have tools, livestock, and wagons, "because that is the way white people make a living."

Instead of accepting Sitting Bull's apology and listening to what he had to say, the commissioners launched an attack. Senator John Logan scolded him for breaking up the previous council and then for accusing the committee members of being drunk. He continued,

> *I want to say further that you are not a great chief of this country, that you have no following, no power, no control, and no right to any control. You are on an Indian reservation merely at the sufferance of the government. You are fed by the government, clothed by the government, your children are educated by the government, and all you have and are today is because of the government. If it were not for the government you would be freezing and starving today in the mountains. I merely say these things to you to notify you that you cannot insult the people of the United States of America or its committees. . . . The government feeds and clothes and educates your children now, and desires to teach you to become farmers, and to civilize you, and make you as white men.*

To speed the process of making the Sioux as white men, the Office of Indian Affairs assigned a man named James McLaughlin to head the agency at Standing Rock. McLaughlin, or White Hair, as the Indians called him, was a veteran of the

An 1888 Frank Leslie's Illustrated Newspaper *woodcut portrait of Major James McLaughlin.* [LOC, USZ62-128094]

Indian Service. He was married to a half-breed Santee woman, and his superiors were confident that he could efficiently destroy the culture of the Sioux and replace it with the white man's civilization. After the departure of the Dawes commission, White Hair McLaughlin attempted to diminish Sitting Bull's influence by dealing with more cooperative Indians such as Chief Gall of the Hunkpapas and Chief John Grass of the Blackfoot Sioux.

White Hair's maneuvers had no effect on Sitting Bull's popularity. All visitors, Indian or white, wanted to meet him. In the summer of 1883, when the Northern Pacific Railroad celebrated the completion of its transcontinental track, one of the officials in charge of ceremonies decided it would be fitting for an Indian chief to be present to make a speech of welcome to the Great Father and other notables. Sitting Bull was the choice—no other Indian was even considered. A young army officer who understood the Sioux language was assigned to work with the chief to prepare a speech. It would be delivered in Sioux and then translated by the officer.

On September 8, Sitting Bull and the young Bluecoat arrived at Bismarck for the big celebration. They rode at the head of a parade and then sat on the speakers' platform. When Sitting Bull was introduced, he arose and began delivering his speech in Sioux. The young officer listened in dismay. Sitting Bull had changed the flowery text of welcome. "I hate all the white people," he was saying. "You are thieves and liars. You have taken away our land and made us outcasts."

Knowing that only the army officer could understand what he was saying, Sitting Bull paused occasionally for applause. He bowed, smiled, and then uttered a few more insults. At last he sat down, and the bewildered interpreter took his place. The officer had only a short translation written out, a few friendly

Sitting Bull's fame brought him many visitors. Here he and his family pose with a white woman, probably the wife of an officer or government official, and her child (second from left). Behind them is a cavalry officer on horseback. [LOC, USZ62-62749]

phrases, but by adding several well-worn Indian metaphors, he brought the audience to its feet with a standing ovation for Sitting Bull. The Hunkpapa chief was so popular that the railroad officials took him to St. Paul, Minnesota, for another ceremony.

During the following summer, the secretary of the interior authorized a tour of 15 American cities for Sitting Bull, and his appearances created such a sensation that

William F. Cody—the famous Buffalo Bill—decided he must add the famous chief to his Wild West Show. The Indian Bureau offered some resistance to the proposal at first, but White Hair McLaughlin was enthusiastic. At Standing Rock, Sitting Bull was a constant symbol of Indian resistance. White Hair would have liked to see him go on tour forever.

In the summer of 1885, Sitting Bull joined Buffalo Bill's Wild West Show, traveling throughout the United States and into Canada. He drew tremendous crowds.

After the season ended, he returned to Standing Rock with two farewell presents from Buffalo Bill—a huge white sombrero and a performing horse. The horse had been trained to sit down and raise one hoof at the crack of a gunshot.

In 1887, Buffalo Bill invited Sitting Bull to accompany his show on a tour of Europe, but the chief declined. "I am needed here," he said. "There is more talk of taking our lands."

The land-grab attempt did not come until the following year, when a commission arrived from Washington with a proposal to carve the Great Sioux Reservation into six smaller reservations, leaving nine million acres open for settlement. The commissioners offered the Indians 50 cents an acre for this land. Sitting Bull immediately went to work to convince Gall and John Grass that the Sioux should not stand for such a swindle. For about a month, the commissioners tried to persuade the Standing Rock Indians that Sitting Bull was misleading them, that the sale was for their benefit, and that if they failed to sign they might lose the land anyway. Only 22 Sioux signed at Standing Rock.

In this 1897 publicity photograph for his Wild West show, William F. "Buffalo Bill" Cody poses with Sitting Bull. Cody got his nickname from his years as a U.S. Army scout and buffalo hunter in the late 1860s and early 1870s. [LOC, USZ62-21207]

After failing to obtain the required three-fourths of signatures at the Crow Creek and Lower Brulé agencies, the commissioners gave up. They returned to Washington and recommended that the government ignore the treaty of 1868 and take the land.

In 1888 the United States government was not quite ready to tear up a treaty, but the following year Congress took the first step toward doing essentially that. The politicians decided to force the Indians to sell a large portion of their reservation out of fear that it would be taken away from them if they refused. Should this scheme work, the government would not have to break the treaty.

General George Crook was the chairman of this new commission. He was authorized to offer the Indians $1.50 per acre. With two politicians, Charles Foster of Ohio and William Warner of Missouri, Crook journeyed to the Great Sioux Reservation in May 1889. He was determined to obtain the required number of adult male signatures. He deliberately chose the Rosebud agency for his first council. Since the assassination of Spotted Tail, the Brulés were split into factions, and Crook believed they were unlikely to offer a united front against signing their land away.

He reckoned without a chief named Hollow Horn Bear, who insisted that the commissioners call all the chiefs of the six agencies together for one council instead of traveling from one to another. "You want to make everything safe here," Hollow Horn Bear said accusingly, "and then go on to the other agencies and tell them we have signed."

Crook replied that the Great Father had ordered the commissioners to consult with the Indians at the different agencies "because it is spring now, and if you all come together at one place, your crops will all suffer."

After nine days of discussion, a majority of the Brulés followed Crook's advice and signed. The first signature on the agreement was that of Crow Dog, the assassin of Spotted Tail.

At Pine Ridge in June, the commissioners had to deal with Red Cloud, who demonstrated his remaining power by surrounding the council with several hundred of his mounted warriors. Even Red Cloud and his loyal lieutenants stood firm, the commissioners managed to secure about half of the Oglalas' signatures. To make up the difference, they moved on to the smaller agencies, obtaining signatures at Lower Brulé, Crow Creek, and Cheyenne River. On July 27, they arrived at Standing Rock. Here the decision would be made. If a majority of the Hunkpapas and Blackfoot Sioux refused to sign, the agreement would fail.

Sitting Bull attended but remained silent. His presence was all that was needed to maintain a solid wall of opposition.

Edward S. Curtis photographed Chief Hollow Horn Bear in 1907. Hollow Horn Bear participated in the Fetterman Massacre. [LOC, USZ62-53674]

John Grass was chief spokesman for the Standing Rock Sioux. "When we had plenty of land," he said, "we could give it to you at your own prices, whatever you had in mind to give, but now we have come down to the small portion there is to spare, and you wish to buy the balance. We are not the ones who are offering our lands for sale. It is the Great Father that is after us to sell the land. That is the reason that the price that is put on the land here we think is not enough, therefore we don't want to sell the land at that price."

After several days of fruitless discussion, Crook realized he could win no converts in general councils. He enlisted James McLaughlin in an effort to convince individual Indians that the government would take their land away if they refused to sell. Sitting Bull remained unyielding. Why should the Indians sell their land in order to save the United States government the embarrassment of breaking a treaty to get it?

White Hair McLaughlin arranged secret meetings with John Grass and convinced him to agree to sell. McLaughlin later said, "Finally we fixed up the speech he was to make receding from his former position gracefully, thus to bring him the active support of the other chiefs and settle the matter."

Without informing Sitting Bull, McLaughlin arranged for a final meeting with the commissioners on August 3. The agent stationed his Indian police in a four-column formation around the council grounds to prevent any interruptions by Sitting Bull or his supporters. John Grass had already delivered his speech when Sitting Bull arrived and forced his way in.

"I would like to say something unless you object to my

speaking, and if you do I will not speak. No one told us of the council, and we just got here," he said.

Crook glanced at McLaughlin. "Did Sitting Bull know that we were going to hold a council?" he asked.

"Yes, sir," McLaughlin lied. "Yes, sir, everybody knew it."

Then John Grass and the chiefs moved forward and signed the agreement. It was all over. The Great Sioux Reservation was broken into small islands. Before Sitting Bull could get away from the grounds, a newspaperman asked him how the Indians felt about giving up their lands.

"Indians!" Sitting Bull shouted. "There are no Indians left but me!"

TWELVE

The Death of Sitting Bull

*Then medicine man tell Indians to send word to all Indians to
keep up dancing and the good time will come.*
—WOVOKA, PAIUTE FOUNDER OF THE GHOST DANCE MOVEMENT

FOR MANY YEARS, white missionaries had tried to persuade
Indians to abandon their tribal religions and convert to
Christianity. Many tribes did. What missionaries did not expect was that some Indians might take the stories of Christ and
the Resurrection and combine them with tribal beliefs to create
a new religion. But in 1889 that is what happened in Nevada.
Word of this new religion traveled east to the reservations of
the Sioux, and in the early fall of 1890, some decided to go to
Nevada and learn about it.

In the Drying Grass Moon, on October 9, 1890, a Minneconjou from the Cheyenne River agency came to Standing Rock to
visit Sitting Bull. His name was Kicking Bear, and he brought
news of the Paiute Messiah, Wovoka, who had founded the
religion of the Ghost Dance.

Kicking Bear told Sitting Bull of how a voice had commanded him to go forth and meet the ghosts of Indians who
were to return and inhabit the earth. On the cars of the Iron

Horse, he and Short Bull and nine other Sioux had traveled far toward the place where the sun sets, traveled until the railroad stopped. There they were met by two Indians they had never seen before, but who greeted them as brothers and gave them meat and bread. They supplied the pilgrims with horses and they rode for four suns until they came to a camp of Fish Eaters (Paiutes) near Pyramid Lake in Nevada.

The Fish Eaters told the visitors that Christ had returned to the earth again. Christ must have sent for them to come there, Kicking Bear said; it was destined to happen. To see the Messiah they had to make another journey to the agency at Walker Lake about 100 miles to the southeast.

For two days, Kicking Bear and his friends waited at Walker Lake with hundreds of other Indians speaking in dozens of different tongues. These Indians had come from many reservations to see the Messiah.

Just before sundown on the third day, Christ appeared, and the Indians made a big fire to throw light on him. Kicking Bear had always thought that Christ was a white man like the missionaries, but this man looked like an Indian. After a while he rose and spoke to the waiting crowd. "I have sent for you and am glad to see you," he said. "I am going to talk to you after a while about your relatives who are dead and gone. My children, I want you to listen to all I have to say to you. I will teach you how to dance a dance, and I want you to dance it. Get ready for your dance, and when the dance is over, I will talk to you." Then he commenced to dance. Soon everybody joined in, the Messiah singing while they danced. They danced the Dance of the Ghosts until late at night, when the Messiah told them they had danced enough.

Next morning, Kicking Bear and the others went up close to the Messiah to see if he had the scars of crucifixion, which the missionaries on the reservations had told them about. There was a scar on his wrist and one on his face, but they could not see his feet because he was wearing moccasins. Throughout the day he talked to them. In the beginning, he said, God made the earth, and then sent Christ to earth to teach the people, but white men had treated him badly, leaving scars on his body, and so he had gone back to heaven. Now he had returned to earth as an Indian, and he was to renew everything as it used to be and make it better.

In the next springtime, when the grass was knee high, the earth would be covered with new soil that would bury all the white men, and the new land would be covered with sweet grass and running water and trees. Great herds of buffalo and wild horses would come back. The Indians who danced the Ghost Dance would be taken up in the air and suspended there while a wave of new earth was passing, and then they would be set down among the ghosts of their ancestors on the new earth, where only Indians would live.

After a few days at Walker Lake, Kicking Bear and his friends learned how to dance the Ghost Dance, and then they mounted their horses to return to the railroad. As they rode along, Kicking Bear said, the Messiah flew above them in the air, teaching them songs for the new dance. At the railroad, he left them, telling them to return to their people and teach what they had

An 1891 Illustrated London News *wood engraving of Sioux Indians performing the Ghost Dance. [LOC, USZ62-52423]*

learned. When the next winter was passed, he would bring the ghosts of their fathers to meet them in the new resurrection.

After returning to Dakota, Kicking Bear had started the new dance at Cheyenne River, Short Bull had brought it to Rosebud, and others were introducing it at Pine Ridge. Big Foot's band of Minneconjous, Kicking Bear said, was made up mostly of women who had lost husbands or other male relatives in battle. They danced until they fainted because they wanted to bring their dead warriors back.

Sitting Bull listened to all that Kicking Bear had to say about the Messiah and the Ghost Dance. He did not believe it was possible for dead men to return and live again, but his people had heard of the Messiah and were fearful he would pass them by and let them disappear when the new resurrection came, unless they joined in the dancing. Sitting Bull had no objections to his people dancing the Ghost Dance, but he had heard that agents at some reservations were bringing soldiers in to stop the ceremonies. He did not want soldiers coming in to frighten, and perhaps shoot guns at, his people. Kicking Bear replied that if the Indians wore the sacred garments of the Messiah—Ghost Shirts painted with magic symbols—no harm could come to them. Not even the bullets of the Bluecoats' guns could penetrate a Ghost Shirt.

With some skepticism, Sitting Bull invited Kicking Bear to remain with his band at Standing Rock and teach them the Dance of the Ghosts. Across the West, on almost every Indian reservation, the Ghost Dance spread like a prairie fire in a high wind. Agitated Indian Bureau inspectors and army officers from Dakota to Arizona, from Indian Territory to Nevada, were scared. Soon the official word was "Stop the Ghost Dancing."

"A more [dangerous] system of religion could not have been offered to a people who stood on the threshold of civilization," White Hair McLaughlin said. Although he was a practicing Catholic, McLaughlin, like most other agents, failed to recognize the Ghost Dance's similarity to the Christian faith.

A week after Kicking Bear came to Standing Rock, White Hair McLaughlin sent a dozen Indian police to remove him from the reservation. Awed by Kicking Bear's aura of holiness, the policemen referred McLaughlin's order to Sitting Bull, but the chief refused to take action. On October 16, McLaughlin sent a larger force of police, and this time Kicking Bear was escorted off the reservation.

The following day McLaughlin notified the commissioner of Indian Affairs that the real power behind the "pernicious system of religion" at Standing Rock was Sitting Bull. He recommended that the chief be arrested, removed from the reservation, and confined to a military prison. The commissioner conferred with the secretary of war, and they decided that such action would create more trouble than it would prevent.

By mid-November, Ghost Dancing was so widespread on the Sioux reservations that almost all other activities came to a halt. Government agents were terrified and pleaded for military help. On November 20, the Indian Bureau in Washington ordered reservation agents to telegraph the names of all the leaders of the disturbances. That list was then transmitted to

Bear Coat Miles's army headquarters in Chicago. Miles saw Sitting Bull's name and immediately assumed that he was to blame.

Meanwhile, at Pine Ridge, the army had already brought in troops, creating a tense situation between the Indians and the military. A former agent, Dr. Valentine McGillycuddy, was sent there to make recommendations for a resolution of the difficulties. "I should let the dance continue," McGillycuddy said. "The coming of the troops has frightened the Indians. If the Seventh-Day Adventists prepare their ascension robes for the second coming of the Savior, the United States Army is not put in motion to prevent them. Why should not the Indians have the same privilege? If the troops remain, trouble is sure to come." This viewpoint, however, was not to prevail. On December 12, Lieutenant Colonel William F. Drum, who was commanding troops at Fort Yates, received orders from General Miles "to secure the person of Sitting Bull."

On December 15, 1890, just before daybreak, 43 Indian police surrounded Sitting Bull's log cabin. Three miles away a squadron of cavalry waited as a support force if needed. Lieutenant Bull Head, the Indian policeman in charge of the party, found Sitting Bull asleep on the floor. When he was awakened, the chief asked, "What do you want here?"

"You are my prisoner," said Bull Head. "You must go to the agency."

Sitting Bull yawned and sat up. "All right," he replied. "Let me put on my clothes, and I'll go with you." He asked the policemen to have his horse saddled.

When Bull Head emerged from the cabin with Sitting Bull, he found a crowd of Ghost Dancers gathering outside. They outnumbered the police four to one. Catch-the-Bear, one of the dancers, moved toward Bull Head. "You think you are going to take him," Catch-the-Bear shouted. "You shall not do it!"

"Come now," Bull Head said quietly to his prisoner, "do not listen to anyone." But Sitting Bull held back, making it necessary for Bull Head and his associate, Sergeant Red Tomahawk, to force him toward his horse.

At this moment, Catch-the-Bear threw off his blanket and brought up a rifle. He fired at Bull Head, wounding him in the side. As Bull Head fell, he tried to shoot his assailant, but the bullet struck Sitting Bull instead. Almost simultaneously, Red Tomahawk shot Sitting Bull through the head and killed him.

This 1891 lithograph from a Chicago printmaking company called Kurz & Allison is titled Capture & Death of Sitting Bull. *It is another example of an inaccurate and romanticized interpretation of an event involving Native Americans. [LOC, DIG-pga-01896]*

Sitting Bull's original grave in Fort Yates, North Dakota, in 1906. In 1953, residents of nearby Mobridge, South Dakota, claimed to have dug up his grave and reburied his remains near their town under a 20-ton block of concrete. They said the purpose was to move him closer to his birthplace. Historians and some Sioux leaders believe that the remains buried in Mobridge were not those of Sitting Bull. [LOC, USZ62-104929]

During the firing, the old show horse that Buffalo Bill had presented to Sitting Bull began to go through his tricks. He sat upright, raised one hoof, and it seemed to those who watched that he was performing the Dance of the Ghosts. When the horse ceased his dancing and wandered away, the wild fighting resumed. Only the arrival of the nearby cavalry detachment saved the Indian police from death.

THIRTEEN

The Massacre at Wounded Knee

We tried to run, but they shot us like we were buffalo.
—Louise Weasel Bear of the Minneconjou Sioux

Had it not been for the Ghost Dance religion, the Sioux in their grief and anger over the assassination of Sitting Bull might have risen up against the guns of the soldiers. But hundreds of now leaderless Hunkpapas fled Standing Rock, seeking refuge in one of the Ghost Dance camps or with the last of the great chiefs, Red Cloud, at Pine Ridge. On the 17th of the Moon when the Deer Shed Their Horns (December), about 100 of these fleeing Hunkpapas reached Big Foot's Minneconjou camp near Cherry Creek. That same day the War Department issued orders for the arrest and imprisonment of Big Foot. He was on the list of "fomenters of disturbances."

As soon as Big Foot learned that Sitting Bull had been killed, he started his people toward Pine Ridge, hoping Red Cloud could protect them from the soldiers. En route, he fell ill with pneumonia. When his lungs began bleeding, he had to travel in a wagon. On December 28, as they neared Porcupine Creek, the Minneconjous sighted four troops of cavalry approaching. Big Foot immediately ordered a white flag raised over his wagon. That afternoon he greeted Major Samuel Whitside, Seventh U.S. Cavalry. Big Foot's blankets were stained with blood, and as he talked in a hoarse whisper with Whitside, red drops fell from his nose and froze in the bitter cold.

Whitside told Big Foot that he had orders to take him to a cavalry camp on Wounded Knee Creek. The Minneconjou chief replied that he was going in that direction. He was taking his people to Pine Ridge for safety.

The major glanced at the ailing chief and then gave an order for his army ambulance to be brought forward. The ambulance would be warmer and would give Big Foot an easier ride than the jolting wagon. After that was done, the combined column renewed its trek.

Twilight was falling when the column reached Chankpe Opi Wakpala, the creek called Wounded Knee. The wintry dusk and the tiny crystals of ice dancing in the dying light added a supernatural quality to the somber landscape.

At the cavalry tent camp on Wounded Knee Creek, the Indians were carefully counted. There were 120 men and 230 women and children. Because of the gathering darkness, Major Whitside decided to wait until morning before disarming his prisoners. He assigned them a camping area immediately to the south of the military camp and issued them rations. As there was a shortage of tepee covers, he gave them several tents. Whitside ordered a stove placed in Big Foot's tent and sent a regimental surgeon to care for the sick chief. To make certain that none of his prisoners escaped, the major stationed two troops of cavalry around the Sioux tepees and then posted his two Hotchkiss guns on top of a rise overlooking the camp. The barrels of these guns, which could hurl explosive charges for more than two miles, were positioned to rake the length of the Indian lodges.

Later in the darkness of that December night, the remainder of the Seventh Regiment marched in from the east and quietly set up camp north of Major Whitside's troops. Colonel James

An 1891 John C. H. Grabill photograph of a unit of troops around a Hotchkiss gun. The Hotchkiss gun was a light, easy-to-use cannon favored by troops at the end of the 19th century. [LOC, DIG-ppmsc-02552]

W. Forsyth, the man who had been given command of Custer's former regiment, now took charge of operations.

After placing two more Hotchkiss guns on the slope beside the others, Forsyth and his officers settled down for the evening with a keg of whiskey to celebrate the capture of Big Foot.

"The following morning there was a bugle call," said Wasumaza, one of Big Foot's warriors. "Then I saw the soldiers mounting their horses and surrounding us. It was announced that all men should come to the center for a talk and that after the talk they were to move on to Pine Ridge agency. Big Foot was brought out of his tepee and sat in front of his tent, and the older men were gathered around him and sitting right near him in the center."

After issuing hardtack biscuits for breakfast rations, Colonel Forsyth informed the Indians that they were now to be disarmed. "They called for guns and arms," White Lance, a member of Big Foot's band, later

This 1913 photograph shows a Sioux camp near the site of the Wounded Knee Massacre. A line of cavalry troops is in the background. [LOC, USZ62-133722]

said, "so all of us gave the guns and they were stacked up in the center." The soldier chiefs were not satisfied with the number of weapons surrendered and sent details of troops to search the tepees. "They would go right into the tents and come out with bundles and tear them open," Dog Chief, another member, said. "They brought our axes, knives, and tent stakes and piled them near the guns."

Still not satisfied, the soldier chiefs ordered the warriors to remove their blankets and submit to searches for weapons. The Indians' faces showed their anger, but only the medicine man, Yellow Bird, made any real protest. He danced a few Ghost Dance steps, and chanted one of the holy songs, assuring the warriors that the soldiers' bullets could not penetrate their sacred garments.

Troopers found only two rifles, one of them a new Winchester belonging to a young Minneconjou named Black Coyote. Black Coyote raised the Winchester above his head, shouting that he paid much money for the rifle and that it belonged to him. Some years afterward, Wasumaza, who had changed his name to Dewey Beard, recalled that Black Coyote was deaf.

If they had left him alone, he was going to put his gun down where he should. They grabbed him and spinned him in the east direction. He was still unconcerned even then. He hadn't his gun pointed at anyone. His intention was to put that gun down. They came on and grabbed the gun that he was going to put down. Right after they spun him around

Wounded
Knee

DAKOTA
TERRITORY

Wounded Knee Creek

✕	Troop positions
⊬	Hotchkiss guns
⅄	Big Foot's camp
⚠	Army camp
﹌	Ridgeline
▨	Roads
～	Creek

Miles
0   1/4   1/2

there was the report of a gun, was quite loud. I couldn't say that anybody was shot, but following that was a crash.

At the sound of the gunshot, the soldiers began firing their weapons. The sound of rifles was deafening, filling the air with powder smoke. Among the dying who lay sprawled on the frozen ground was Big Foot. Then there was a brief lull in the rattle of arms, with small groups of Indians and soldiers

This map shows the location of Big Foot's camp and the surrounding cavalry positions just before the Wounded Knee Massacre occurred.

grappling at close quarters, using knives, clubs, and pistols. As few of the Indians had arms, they soon had to flee. Then the big Hotchkiss guns on the hill opened up on them, raking the Indian camp, shredding the tepees with flying shrapnel, killing men, women, and children.

When the madness ended, Big Foot and more than half of his people were dead or seriously wounded. One estimate placed the final total of dead at nearly 300 of the original 350 men, women, and children. Twenty-five soldiers were dead and 39 wounded, most of them struck by their own bullets or shrapnel.

After the wounded cavalrymen started for the agency at Pine Ridge, a detail of soldiers went over the Wounded Knee site, gathering up Indians who were still alive and loading them into wagons. Since a blizzard was approaching, the dead Indians were left where they had fallen. After the blizzard, when a burial party returned to Wounded Knee, they found the bodies, including Big Foot's, frozen into grotesque shapes.

The wagonloads of wounded Sioux, four men and 47 women and children, reached Pine Ridge after dark. Because the barracks were filled with soldiers, they were left lying in the open wagons in the bitter cold while an inept army officer searched for shelter. Finally the Episcopal mission was opened, the benches taken out, and hay scattered over the rough flooring.

Orlando Scott Goff photographed the ravine where the Wounded Knee Massacre occurred about three weeks after the event. Some of the bodies can be seen in the background. [LOC, USC62-42550]

Another photograph by Orlando Scott Goff of the aftermath of the massacre at Wounded Knee. About three weeks after it happened, a burial party arrived to gather those who had been killed. In the foreground are some of the bodies, covered with blankets.
[LOC, DIG-ppmsca-15849]

It was the fourth day after Christmas 1890. When the first torn and bleeding bodies were carried into the candlelit church, those who were conscious saw Christmas greenery hanging from the open rafters. Above the pulpit was strung a banner: PEACE ON EARTH, GOOD WILL TO MEN.

EPILOGUE

Bittersweet Victory

And I can see that something else died there in the bloody mud
and was buried in the blizzard. A people's dream died there.

—BLACK ELK OF THE OGLALA SIOUX

THE UNITED STATES ARMY AWARDED the Medal of Honor to 17 soldiers who participated in the fighting at Wounded Knee. Eventually three more soldiers would receive the decoration, bringing the total to 20. At the time, the Medal of Honor was the only award for military valor, and its standards were not as strict as they later became. The policy then was that conduct deserving the Medal of Honor "should not be the simple discharge of duty, but such acts beyond this." Those acts were not identified.

The official descriptions of the awards for Wounded Knee typically included such phrases as "extraordinary gallantry," "distinguished conduct," and "distinguished bravery."

Though other tribes would continue to observe the Ghost Dance for several years—and one tribe practices it to this day—the massacre at Wounded Knee ended its influence among the Sioux.

On December 10, 1909, Mahpiua-luta, Red Cloud, went to the bosom of the Great Spirit. It was believed he was 90 years old. During the last three years of his life, he had been blind and in declining health. He had outlived all the other Sioux chiefs who had fought the Bluecoats. He had also outlived Chief Joseph and Geronimo, two great chiefs from other Indian nations who had fought in vain to defend their people and land from the United States. Chief Joseph of the Nez Percés died in 1904. It was to fight his warriors that the Bluecoats enlisted the Oglalas from Crazy Horse's band, sparking the event that resulted in Crazy Horse's death. The Apache chief Geronimo, the last chief to surrender to the Bluecoats, died the same year as Red Cloud, on February 17. Only the Comanche chief Quanah Parker, the half-breed son of a Comanche chief and a white woman, outlived him, dying two years later, on February 23, 1911.

When the 20th century began, the United States government was well along the road to "reforming" the Indian nations. *Reforming* was the word used to describe the effort to make all Indians adopt a "civilized" lifestyle. Reformers both inside and outside the government saw tribal society and traditional Indian culture as roadblocks to the Indians' survival. Therefore they decided that the only way to save these Indians was to unmake them as Indians and remake them as white men. The main instrument of their authority to do this was the General Allotment Act of 1887, also known as the Dawes Act or the Dawes Severalty Act, after its sponsor Senator Henry L. Dawes. Without consulting the tribes, the government said Indian land could no longer be owned by the tribe as a whole. Instead, like the white man's land, it would be divided into pieces and each member of the tribe would be "allotted" one portion that he or she would individually own. This was similar to the homestead system used to give white families free land to settle and farm. The maximum size of the parcels of land was 160 acres, which was given to adult males. Other members received smaller amounts of land portioned in different sizes. If there was any reservation land left after all the tribal members had received their allotment, that "surplus" land was sold to whites. The money from the sale was then held in trust by the government, and the interest earned was used to support the tribe.

Not only did the government take more land from the tribes during this period, it also took thousands of their children.

Ever since the arrival of the first white settlers to the American continents, missionaries had worked not only to convert Indians to Christianity but also to educate them. During the late 1800s, the United States government stepped in and sponsored schools in or by reservations. The government became active because it wanted to speed up the assimilation process—integrating the Sioux and other Indians into white society. While tribal parents recognized that it was necessary for their children to get a white man's education to help them deal with the white men and their ways, they and their children resisted all attempts to eliminate their tribal culture and traditions.

Frustrated by this, the government decided that the only way assimilation would happen was to physically remove the children from their parents and send them to boarding schools far away from the reservations. The first and most famous of these boarding schools was the Carlisle Indian Industrial School, established in 1879 in an abandoned military barracks in Carlisle, Pennsylvania. Eventually a total of 26 off-reservation government-sponsored boarding schools were created.

The Indian boarding school program was a 12-year education system designed to force-feed a new way of life to the children of the different tribes. The children led a strict and regimented life. They were forbidden to speak their native languages. Their hair was cut in the fashion of white men and women. They had to wear uniforms. They were punished for breaking even the most minor of rules. Many children hated the schools. Scores ran away and attempted to return to their reservations and families. Some died, usually after having contracted a contagious white man's disease such as measles, which was deadly to Indians because they had no immunity. Once the children graduated from the schools, they returned to the reservation. Many later did what the government hoped and settled in cities outside their reservations.

Over time, the boarding school system was criticized for being harsh and cruel. Finally, in the 1920s, the last of these schools was closed.

Meanwhile the allotment system attempted to make white farmers out of the Sioux on land that was unsuitable for farming. The result was a disaster that left many Sioux starving and in poverty. In 1887 the Sioux and other Indian nations of the Great Plains held about 138 million acres. When the government ended the Dawes Act in 1934, Indian holdings had shrunk to 52 million acres.

But the government was not done. Over the next four decades, the federal government tried a variety of approaches to force assimilation. The last program, started in 1953 and lasting about 10 years, was designed to end the federal government's responsibility for the social and economic welfare of the tribes and their lands.

But by now the Sioux and other tribes and Native American nations had learned enough of the white man's ways to fight back using the white man's own weapons of laws and courts. In 1944, representatives from 50 tribes, most from the Plains Indians, met in Denver, Colorado, and formed the National Congress of American Indians. This organization forced the federal government to end its termination policy and to recognize an Indian policy of "self-determination" that gave the tribes more say over their lives and preserved their culture. It has grown to include 250 tribes and continues to advocate for Indian rights, environmental protection, and natural resources management, as well as the protection of Indian cultures and religious freedom.

In 1968, a more radical and militant Native American activist organization was formed, the American Indian Movement (AIM). In 1973, the Pine Ridge Reservation chapter of AIM led by Russell Means and Dennis Banks made national headlines spotlighting the plight of the Sioux. And they did it at Wounded Knee.

Suffering from extreme poverty, racial prejudice from the local white community, and political corruption from the tribal government itself, the Pine Ridge Reservation was an example of how poor conditions were for tribes in general, and the Sioux at Pine Ridge in particular. AIM supported an effort to unseat tribal chairman Dick Wilson, and this effort escalated into numerous violent outbreaks. An attempt to legally remove Wilson from office failed under controversial circumstances. In protest, on February 27, 1973, AIM and Wilson's opponents occupied Wounded Knee. A combined force of U.S. marshals, FBI agents, Bureau of Indian Affairs police, Wilson's tribal police, and military troops surrounded the hamlet. The siege became headline news nationwide. After negotiations lasting 71 days, and after two AIM supporters had been killed and a U.S. marshal seriously wounded, the siege was lifted. Banks and Means were arrested and charged with a wide range of crimes ranging from auto theft to criminal conspiracy. The trial lasted more than eight months. In his decision, U.S. District Court Chief Justice Fred Nichol wrote, "I am forced to the conclusion that the prosecution in this trial had something other than attaining justice foremost in its mind. . . ." He added that misconduct by federal prosecutors "formed a pattern throughout the course of the trial." All charges against Dennis Banks and Russell Means were dropped. Conditions at Pine Ridge continued to remain poor and did not begin to improve until years had passed.

Unlike the National Congress of American Indians, AIM did not have a strong central organization, and in the years following Wounded Knee, it fell into decline. By the 1980s, it was no longer a national organization.

In June 1974, at the Standing Rock Reservation that straddles the border of North and South Dakota, the Sioux hosted the International Indian Treaty Council. It was attended by 5,000 representatives from 98 Native American nations in North and South America. When the council concluded, it issued a declaration establishing an independent Oglala nation and asserting the rights of Native peoples. It specifically charged the United States with "gross violations" of its treaties with Native American nations. One treaty in the list of broken treaties was the 1868 Treaty of Fort Laramie. In 1977, the United Nations gave the organization formal recognition. The International Indian Treaty Council has since grown to become a vocal organization for the rights of Native peoples around the world.

Then in 1980, 103 years after Congress had seized Paha Sapa, the Sioux nation had its decisive day in court. In 1877, Congress tore up the 1868 Treaty of Fort Laramie and took the Black Hills. In 1917, the Sioux Nation began the legal fight to regain Paha Sapa. One early lower-court decision in the Sioux Nation's favor awarded it more than $17 million plus interest dating back to 1877. But the government fought the ruling, and the case slowly worked its way up to the highest court in the United States, the Supreme Court.

On June 30, 1980, in the case *United States v. Sioux Nation of Indians*, the Supreme Court ruled eight to one that Congress was wrong when it took the Black Hills in 1877. It said that the Sioux Nation should receive a fair price for the land, plus 103 years' worth of interest. The Sioux Nation has said that it does not want money. It wants the return of Paha Sapa.

On December 17, 2007, Russell Means led a group called the Lakota Freedom Delegation to Washington, D.C. The delegation delivered a statement to the federal government, stating that it

Montana

North Dakota

Minnesota

Republic of Lakotah

South Dakota

Wisconsin

Wyoming

Iowa

Colorado

Nebraska

Illinois

Kansas

Missouri

This map shows the location of the proposed Republic of Lakotah and the parts of the five states that would compose it.

had the legal claim to about 77,000 square miles of land in North Dakota, South Dakota, Nebraska, Wyoming, and Montana and that its goal was to establish an independent Republic of Lakotah with that land. Since then Means and other leaders have repeatedly called for the return of tribal lands. In March 2010, these Sioux leaders submitted a report to the UN Human Rights Council listing ongoing violations of the terms of the 1851 and 1868 treaties of Fort Laramie by the United States. They also repeated its demand to the president and the secretary of state that the government withdraw from their homeland.

Meanwhile, the special account set aside to pay the Sioux for Paha Sapa is more than $750 million, and growing.

*They made us many promises, more than I can remember,
but they never kept but one: they promised to take our land,
and they took it.*

—RED CLOUD

Time Line

1851

JULY 23 — Treaty of Traverse des Sioux signed between the U.S. Government and the Wahpeton and Santee Sioux.

AUGUST 5 — Treaty of Mendota signed between the U.S. Government and the Mdewakanton and Wahpekute Sioux.

1862

AUGUST 17 — Little Crow's War starts when four hungry Sioux warriors make a raid in Acton Township, Minnesota.

AUGUST 23 — The Battle of New Ulm. After an initial attack four days earlier, the Sioux make a second effort to capture the village. The battle ends in a draw.

SEPTEMBER 23 — The Battle of Birch Coulee. The battle ends in a draw.

SEPTEMBER 26 — Two thousand Santee Sioux surrender. Military court trials against them begin.

NOVEMBER 5 — Sioux trials end with 303 Santees being sentenced to death. Sixteen receive prison terms.

DECEMBER 6 — President Lincoln orders that 39 Sioux may be executed.

DECEMBER 26 — After one Santee Sioux is granted a pardon, 38 Sioux are executed by hanging. Two of those executed were not on the execution list.

1863

JULY 3 — Little Crow is shot and killed by settlers near Acton Township, Minnesota.

1865

JULY 4 — General Patrick E. Connor starts his campaign against the Sioux, Cheyenne, and Arapaho tribes living in the Powder River country.

AUGUST 28	The Battle of Tongue River, an Arapaho defeat.
1866	
JUNE 5	Peace conference begins between U.S. government representatives and the Sioux led by Red Cloud. Its purpose is to open the Bozeman Trail that cuts through the Powder River country.
JUNE 13	Troops led by Colonel Henry Carrington arrive at Fort Laramie planning to build forts on the Bozeman Trail even though the treaty granting them the right to do so has not yet been signed.
JUNE 14	Red Cloud breaks off negotiations. The Indians leave Fort Laramie, and the conference ends in failure.
JULY 13	Construction of Fort Phil Kearny begins in the disputed Powder River country.
DECEMBER 21	The Fetterman Massacre—or the Battle of the Hundred Slain—a Sioux, Cheyenne, and Arapaho victory.
1867	
AUGUST 1	The Hayfield Battle is fought between Cheyenne and U.S. cavalry followed by the Wagon Box Battle between the Sioux and U.S. cavalry the next day. Both battles end in a draw.
SEPTEMBER 19	A peace delegation led by General William T. Sherman arrives at Platte City, Nebraska, to try to restart treaty negotiations. Red Cloud refuses to attend.
NOVEMBER 9	General Sherman's delegation arrives at Fort Laramie. Red Cloud again refuses to attend. After a few days of parleys with lesser chiefs that go nowhere, the peace commission leaves, having failed to sign a new treaty.
1868	
JULY 29	U.S. Army troops abandon Fort C. F. Smith, one of the forts on the Bozeman Trail. Red Cloud and his warriors burn it to the ground. A month later, the army abandons Fort Phil Kearny and the Cheyenne destroy it.

Young-Man-Afraid-of-His-Horses.
[LOC, USZ62-121245]

NOVEMBER 6	Red Cloud signs the Treaty of Fort Laramie (1868) that recognizes Sioux ownership of the Powder River region, the Paha Sapa (Black Hills), and the surrounding areas.
1874	
JULY 2	In a violation of the terms of the Treaty of Fort Laramie (1868), Lieutenant Colonel George Armstrong Custer leads a gold-hunting expedition into the Paha Sapa and returns with the announcement that the Black Hills are filled with gold. Gold miners soon arrive by the hundreds.
1875	
SEPTEMBER 20	A commission arrives at Camp Robinson, Nebraska, with orders to buy the Black Hills from the Sioux. About a week later, the commission leaves in failure.
DECEMBER 3	Commissioner of Indian Affairs Edward P. Smith orders all nonreservation Indians to voluntarily report to agencies by January 31, 1876, or "military force would be sent to compel them."
1876	
JANUARY 31	Commissioner Smith's deadline passes without any nonreservation Indians arriving. Because of heavy snow and severe winter weather, many bands did not receive the news by the deadline.
FEBRUARY 7	Secretary of War William W. Belknap authorizes General Philip Sheridan to begin military operations against the "hostile Sioux."
MARCH 17	Troops under the command of Colonel Joseph J. Reynolds attack a mixed Cheyenne and Sioux camp on the Little Powder River. The camp is destroyed, but most Indians escape and join Crazy Horse in his camp.
JUNE 17	The Battle of the Rosebud—known to the Indians as the Battle Where the Girl Saved Her Brother—is fought, ending in a Sioux and Cheyenne victory.
JUNE 25	The Battle of Little Bighorn, the greatest victory by American Indians against the U.S. Army.

| OCTOBER 20 | Colonel Nelson Miles meets with Sitting Bull to try to persuade Sitting Bull to surrender and live on a reservation. Sitting Bull refuses, and the Battle of Cedar Creek is fought the next day. In the spring of 1877 Sitting Bull takes his band up into Canada. |

1877

JANUARY 8	Battle of Wolf Mountain. Crazy Horse and his warriors defeat a cavalry force led by Colonel Miles.
APRIL 14	A large group of Sioux led by Chief Touch-the-Clouds surrenders to the U.S. Army.
APRIL 27	Red Cloud meets Crazy Horse and persuades him to bring his followers to Camp Robinson and surrender.
AUGUST 31	Angry that some of his warriors are joining the U.S. Army to help fight Nez Percé, Crazy Horse rejects the government offer of a reservation and plans to leave.
SEPTEMBER 5	Crazy Horse is captured and killed by U.S. Army soldiers at Chief Spotted Tail's reservation in Dakota Territory.
OCTOBER 17	General Alfred Terry goes to Fort Walsh, Canada, to persuade Sitting Bull to return to the United States. The meeting ends in failure.

1881

| JULY 19 | After four years of exile in Canada, Sitting Bull and 186 remaining followers arrive at Fort Buford, Dakota Territory. Though promised a pardon if he returned, Sitting Bull is imprisoned at Fort Randall. |
| AUGUST 5 | Spotted Tail is killed by Crow Dog. Many Sioux believe it is a plot created by the U.S. government to split the Sioux leadership. |

1883

| MAY 18 | The first in a series of three government commissions begins to investigate suspicious claims of new Sioux land purchases by a group of whites led by Reverend Samuel D. Hinman. The most important commission was led by Senator Henry L. Dawes. All discover that the group lied, and the sale is stopped. |

193

1889

JULY 27   General George Crook and a commission arrive at the Standing Rock Sioux reservation in Dakota Territory and trick the Sioux into selling nine million acres of land to the government.

1890

OCTOBER 9   Kicking Bear, a Minneconjou, visits Sitting Bull and brings him word of the new Ghost Dance religion. So many Sioux become followers that the U.S. government becomes alarmed.

NOVEMBER 20   The Office of Indian Affairs in Washington, D.C., orders reservation agents to provide a list of names of Ghost Dance leaders. One of the names on the list is Sitting Bull.

DECEMBER 12   Lieutenant Colonel William F. Drum receives orders to arrest Sitting Bull.

DECEMBER 15   Sitting Bull is shot and killed by agency policemen when Ghost Dance followers try to prevent his arrest.

DECEMBER 17   The War Department orders the arrest of Chief Big Foot of the Minneconjou, who is accused of being a Ghost Dance leader.

DECEMBER 28   Big Foot and his followers are captured by a cavalry force led by Major Samuel Whitside. They are ordered to make camp near Wounded Knee Creek, Dakota Territory.

DECEMBER 29   The Wounded Knee Massacre. Cavalry troops fire on the mostly unarmed Sioux. As many as 300 are killed. The massacre ends the influence of the Ghost Dance on the Sioux nation.

1909

DECEMBER 10   Red Cloud dies of natural causes.

Glossary

AGENCY. An administrative department within the U.S. government that provides goods and services to reservation Native Americans. Also refers to land set aside for their use. See RESERVATION.

ALLIANCE. An agreement between different groups that unites them for a common purpose.

AMBUSH. A surprise attack by people who were hiding in a concealed position.

ANNUITY. A sum of money paid once a year.

APPROPRIATION. The setting aside or assigning of something, such as money, for specific purposes.

ASSIMILATION. Integrating a smaller, usually ethnic, group into a larger one and causing it to lose its identity.

BREASTWORKS. A protective barrier that is chest high.

BUFFALO. This symbol of the American West is properly named the North American bison. It got the name *buffalo* because it reminded European explorers of African and Asian buffalo.

CASUALTY. A person killed or wounded in battle.

CAVALRY. Soldiers who fight on horseback.

CESSION. A formal giving up of rights or property, usually through the signing of a treaty.

COLUMN. In the military, a line of troops moving in the same direction.

COMPLIANT. Willing to agree or to obey the rules of others.

CONDUCT. The way a person acts or behaves.

COULEE. A streambed or small ravine.

DIPLOMACY. The act of dealing with people in a sensitive way in order to reach an agreement or avoid conflict.

FORAGING. Searching for food in a large area.

GUERRILLA. A person who takes part in irregular fighting, often through hit-and-run raids, rather than participating in an organized military campaign.

HOWITZER. A short-barreled cannon that shoots shells in a high arc.

INFANTRY. Soldiers who march and fight on foot.

LANCE. A spear.

MARAUDING. Making attacks for the purpose of stealing things, damaging property, or intimidating people.

MILITIA. A force of civilians organized in an emergency to fight an enemy.

MULATTO. A person of mixed white and black ancestry.

MUTINY. An open rebellion against authorities.

PARLEY. A meeting between two opposing groups in an attempt to reach a peaceful agreement.

PEMMICAN. A concentrated, dried food consisting of lean meat and fat.

PENITENTIARY. A prison.

PROSPECTOR. A person who searches land for minerals, usually gold.

RELINQUISHMENT. The releasing or letting go of something.

RENDEZVOUS. To meet at a particular place and time.

RESERVATION. Land set aside for the use of Native Americans. See AGENCY.

RICOCHET. To bounce one or more times off something; also something (like a bullet) that ricochets.

STOCKADE. A wall formed by upright posts and designed for defense against attack.

SUBJECTION. A state of being controlled or dominated through the use of force.

TANGIBLE. Real, clearly seen, touched, or understood.

TRAVOIS. A type of sled made of two poles and strapped to a horse or dog used by Plains Indians to carry possessions.

The Sioux Calendar

A Teton warrior performing a vision ceremony.
[LOC, USZ62-99611]

THE CALENDAR USED TODAY BY the United States and many other nations is the Gregorian calendar. It is named after Pope Gregory XIII and was started in 1582. Before that, many civilizations—including Native American peoples—used what was called a lunar calendar, based on the cycles of the moon. The names of the different months described the seasons or the growth and changes in plant and animal life at that time of year. Because the names of the months were based on what the tribes experienced, it was common for a month to have more than one name. This was particularly true with the Sioux, some of whom lived in forests while others lived in open prairie. Also, sometimes translators would interpret the name slightly differently, causing a change in a word or two of a month's name. It's also worth noting that the Native American calendars did not have any days in them, only months, and some months share the same name. Here, the names of the months in the Sioux calendar are presented in relation to the months of the Gregorian calendar.

January
Moon of Strong Cold
Moon of Frost on the Tepees
Moon When the Wolves Run Together

February
Moon of the Dark Red Calves
Raccoon Moon

March
Moon of the Snowblind
Moon When Buffalo Cows Drop Their Calves
Sore Eye Moon

April
Geese Laying Moon
Moon of the Red Grass Appearing
Moon of the Greening Grass

May	Moon When the Ponies Shed
June	Strawberry Moon Moon of Making Fat Moon When the Grass Is Up
July	Moon of the Red Blooming Lilies Moon of the Red Cherries Moon When the Cherries Are Ripe
August	Moon When the Geese Shed Their Feathers Moon When the Cherries Turn Black Moon When the Chokecherries Are Ripe
September	Drying Grass Moon Moon When the Calves Grow Hair Moon When the Plums Are Scarlet
October	Moon of Falling Leaves Moon of Changing Seasons Drying Grass Moon
November	Deer Rutting Moon Moon of Falling Leaves
December	Moon of Popping Trees Moon When the Deer Shed Their Horns Moon When Buffalo Cow's Fetus Is Getting Large

Fort Snelling as seen from the opposite riverbank where the Minnesota River joins the Mississippi River. [LOC, D4-4685]

Recommended Reading

Ambrose, Stephen E. *Crazy Horse and Custer: The Parallel Lives of Two American Warriors.* New York, NY: Anchor Books, 1996.

Brown, Dee. *Bury My Heart at Wounded Knee: An Indian History of the American West.* New York, NY: Holt Paperbacks, 2007.

———. *The Fetterman Massacre.* Lincoln, NE: Bison Books, 1970.

Greene, Jerome A., editor. *Lakota and Cheyenne: Indian Views of the Great Sioux War, 1876–1877.* Norman, OK: University of Oklahoma Press, 1994.

Hedren, Paul L. *Traveler's Guide to the Great Sioux War: The Battlefields, Forts, and Related Sites of America's Greatest Indian War.* Helena, MT: Montana Historical Society Press, 1996.

McPherson, James M. *Into the West: From Reconstruction to the Final Days of the American Frontier.* New York, NY: Atheneum, 2006.

Michno, Gregory F. *Encyclopedia of Indian Wars: Western Battles and Skirmishes 1850–1890.* Missoula, MT: Mountain Press Publishing, 2003.

Paul, R. Eli, editor. *Autobiography of Red Cloud: War Leader of the Oglalas.* Helena, MT: Montana Historical Society Press, 1997.

Philbrick, Nathaniel. *The Last Stand: Custer, Sitting Bull, and the Battle of the Little Bighorn.* New York, NY: Viking, 2010.

Sandoz, Mari. *These Were the Sioux.* Lincoln, NE: Bison Books, 1985.

Stanley, George Edward. *Sitting Bull: Great Sioux Hero.* New York, NY: Sterling Publishing, 2010.

Utley, Robert M. *The Lance and the Shield: The Life and Times of Sitting Bull.* New York, NY: Ballantine Books, 1994.

Utley, Robert M., and Wilcomb E. Washburn. *Indian Wars.* New York, NY: Mariner Books, 2002.

Suggested Websites

Additional information about the Sioux, including how to speak their language, can be found on the following websites:

AMERICAN INDIAN MOVEMENT
www.aimovement.org
The official website of the American Indian Movement.

CARLISLE INDIAN INDUSTRIAL SCHOOL HISTORY
http://home.epix.net/~landis/histry.html
A site that presents the history of the Carlisle Indian Industrial School and the Indian boarding school program.

DAILY LIFE IN OLDEN TIMES: THE SIOUX NATION
http://nativeamericans.mrdonn.org/plains/Sioux.html
A website designed for middle school students that covers every aspect of Sioux life and history.

DAKOTA-LAKOTA SIOUX LANGUAGE
www.native-languages.org/dakota.htm
A home page with links to sites designed for middle school students and devoted to the Sioux language, culture, history, legends, and other facts.

INTERNATIONAL INDIAN TREATY COUNCIL
www.treatycouncil.org
The official website of the International Indian Treaty Council. It is an extensive website that spotlights issues affecting Native peoples and the environment throughout the world.

Lakhota.com
www.lakhota.com
An educational site that provides online resources about Sioux culture, heritage, language, and history.

Native American People/Tribes: The Great Sioux Nation
www.snowwowl.com/peoplesioux.html
A general history site about the Sioux and some of its famous chiefs and holy men, with links to other Native American sites.

NCAI
www.ncai.org
The official website for the National Congress of American Indians. It contains information about the organization's history and about modern issues affecting Native Americans.

Republic of Lakotah
www.republicoflakotah.com
The official website of the Republic of Lakotah. It contains news and information about civil rights issues, humanitarian efforts, and issues related to establishing the Republic of Lakotah as an independent country.

Sioux Reservation Websites

Below is a list of the Sioux reservations in the United States and Canada that have websites. Note that the name of the reservation is often taken from a landmark feature such as a ridge, lake, or river. These sites contain information about the Sioux in general, as well as items of interest that deal specifically with the individual reservation, including tribal government, programs, and upcoming events.

Cheyenne River Sioux Tribe
www.sioux.org

Flandreau Santee Sioux Tribe
www.fsst.org

Sitting Bull's family. Standing, from left: Lodge in Sight, Seen By Her Nation, Standing Holy, and Holy Robes. The boy sitting is believed to be William Sitting Bull. [LOC, USZ62-115472]

FORT PECK TRIBES
www.fortpecktribes.org

LOWER BRULÉ SIOUX TRIBE
www.lbst.org

LOWER SIOUX INDIAN COMMUNITY
www.lowersioux.com

OGLALA SIOUX TRIBE
http://home.comcast.net/~zebrec/

PRAIRIE ISLAND INDIAN COMMUNITY
www.prairieisland.org

ROSEBUD SIOUX TRIBE
www.rosebudsiouxtribe-nsn.gov

SANTEE SIOUX TRIBE OF NEBRASKA
www.santeedakota.org/santee_sioux_tribe_of_nebraska.htm

SHAKOPEE MDEWAKANTON SIOUX COMMUNITY
www.shakopeedakota.org

SIOUX VALLEY DAKOTA NATION
www.dakotanation.com

SPIRIT LAKE TRIBE
www.spiritlakenation.com

STANDING ROCK SIOUX TRIBE
www.standingrock.org

UPPER SIOUX COMMUNITY
www.uppersiouxcommunity-nsn.gov

WHITECAP DAKOTA FIRST NATION
www.whitecapdakota.com

⊕ *Index*

(Page references in *italic* refer to illustrations.)

31901055786463